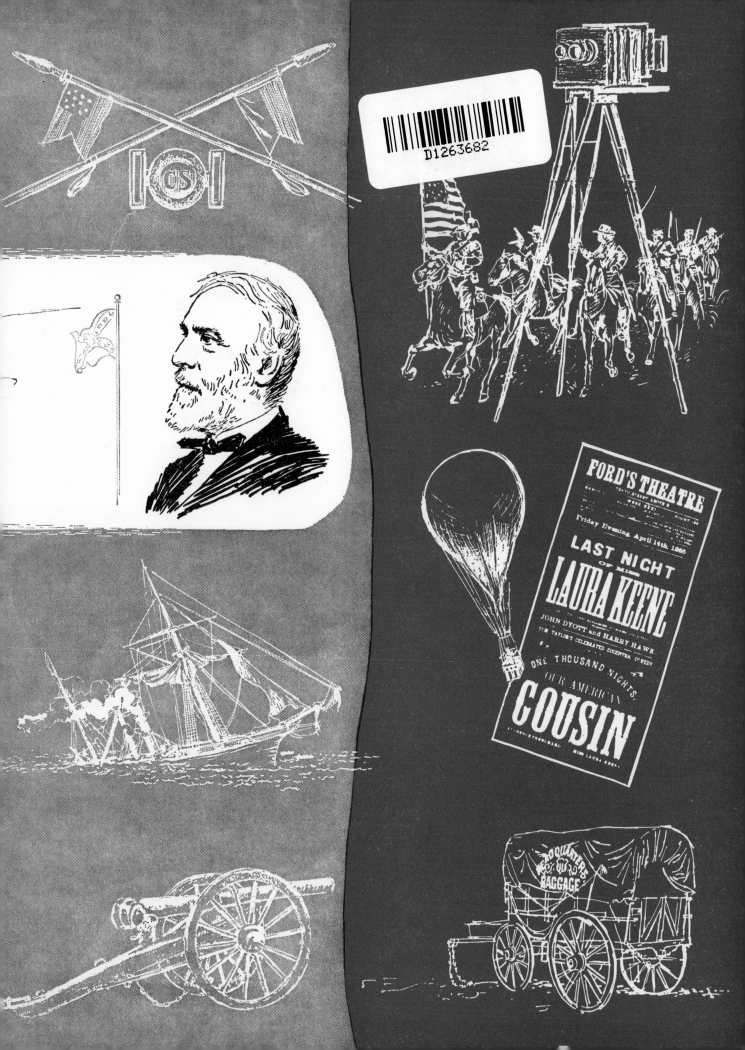

FORD'S THEATRE

Friday Evening, April 14th 1865

LAST NIGHT
OF MISS

LAURA KEENE

JOHN DYOTT and HARRY HAWK

ONE THOUSAND NIGHTS,
OUR AMERICAN

COUSIN

Two Flags Flying

Two

Flags Flying

by Donald J. Sobol

Preface by Ralph Newman

Illustrations by Jerry Robinson

PLATT & MUNK, *Publishers*

NEW YORK

for Rose in love

PUBLISHER'S NOTE

THIS BOOK is *not* a chronological account of the Civil War, a day-to-day rendering. It is not intended to be.

It is instead an array of episodic biographies of fifty important figures of that awesome conflict—twenty-five of the North, twenty-five of the South: men, women, machines; statesmen and soldiers, society belles, assassins, sea marauders, and female spies, some of them all but forgotten in history.

Here, too, is an unexpected foretaste of war that later generations would come to know all too well—war under the sea and in the air.

History records a specific date on which the War Between the States began and the date on which it ended. But events between these two mileposts of history created a pattern in which, very often, there seemed to be no pattern at all. Events and battles, tragedy and turmoil, flowed almost formlessly one into the other.

The author tells us at the outset about The First Shot, and he concludes with General Lee calling upon General Grant at Appomattox. But events described here often occurred simultaneously, or overlapped. Even as in history itself, there is not always a sharp leaving off and a fresh start to every moment or day.

Each chapter of this book, then, is a single biography, complete in itself. Together, these fifty chapters are the chronicle of a time when brother fought brother, when for four long and terrible years—over a people that scarcely a century before had struggled together for their independence—there were Two Flags Flying.

CONTENTS

Following each chapter will be found brief biographical data about the individual involved, together with a short description of the illustrated motif of each chapter.

PREFACE

Ralph Newman, whose preface appears on this page, is recognized internationally as an authority on the Civil War. He is the author, coauthor or editor of numerous books on the subject. His interests, stemming from an early fascination with the history of the land of Lincoln in which he grew up, have brought him into countless, related activities. In 1940, he founded the Civil War Round Table in Chicago; similar groups now exist in almost 100 American cities and abroad. He is proprietor of the Abraham Lincoln Book Shop of Chicago, president of the Illinois State Historical Society, and a member of the advisory board of the national Civil War Centennial Commission, appointed by the President of the United States.

THIS IS A NEW APPROACH to the most thrilling and meaningful of all dramas of the American past. It introduces the reader to this era and to the principal dramatis personae. The spirit and the meaning of the times are here expressed in terms of the people who lived this drama.

Both Thomas Carlyle and Ralph Waldo Emerson have told us that there really is no such thing as history, only biography—that men and women make events. This fact is dramatically demonstrated in the Civil War, the four tragic years that form the narrow neck of the hour glass of our national existence.

Many theories have been advanced as to why, in the almost two hundred years of the existence of this Republic, we focus more attention on these times of trial in the 1860's than on any other era in the American story. Here, as Bruce Catton reminds us, is the only sustained span of tragedy in our history.

I suspect one of the reasons for our fascination with the Civil War is the incredible cast of characters in that drama. We fought the last old-fashioned and the first modern war at the same time. In many respects this was the last great war in which the solitary individual was an important factor. The personal exploits of a Jeb Stuart could have a profound effect on the ultimate outcome of a campaign.

This is an almost incredible tale of actual people and events. The reader's journey into history will prove thrilling, the hunt exciting, and the result rewarding.

RALPH NEWMAN

FOREWORD

SEVERAL MONTHS before this book was completed, there died in Texas a man named Walter Williams, who claimed to be the last veteran of the Civil War. He had fought for the Confederacy, he said, and at the end he had given his age as 117.

With him—or with some veteran already dead—slipped away our last living connection with the war. Never again can a boy sit at the feet of a wrinkled old soldier and hear such words as "I rode with Stuart." Never can he tingle to a brushed-up tale.

The last pair of eyes is closed, the last memory has faded. All that remains is the record. The flesh and the blood are in the earth. A hundred years have passed over the deeds of the Blue and the Gray.

But those who took part in the furious American drama will never truly be gone.

They do not linger in the cobwebs of an attic trunk, or in a rusty medal, or even in the image on a yellow photograph.

They tramp in Virginia when the August sun turns the back roads to smoky dust. They charge in the rustle of leaves at Gettysburg when a father takes his small son by the hand and they walk the sloping route of Pickett's men.

They are with us still, our forebears, marching to the ring of distant trumpets and the roll of history's drums. If we pause and ponder, we can hear them and see them all again.

DONALD J. SOBOL

Eastchester, New York
May, 1960

THE Union had been forged in the fire of freedom. At first, there were only the original thirteen colonies—and they had weathered the myriad trials of a nation's infancy.

Now, eighty years later, the Union had grown to thirty-four states. Twice in this time, the Union had faced the dangers of dissolution, the threat of break-up. In 1832, as the climax of bitter debate over the right of a state to nullify a federal law, President Jackson had come down hard on South Carolina, and thus preserved the Union. In 1850, Henry Clay's compromise had held onto the slave states.

There were men who said that all Jackson and Clay had really achieved was delay. Northern industrial might, they said, was overriding Southern economic, political, and cultural freedom. To preserve its society, which rested on farming and in turn on the labor of slaves, the outnumbered Southern states would have to be independent.

At first there was just the talk, and the words were old and familiar: secession by peaceful, lawful means.

In the North, abolitionists proclaimed the evils of human bondage. Mrs. Harriet Beecher Stowe's UNCLE TOM'S CABIN sold ten thousand copies a week and played to packed theatres.

Then John Brown, who had moved from his native Connecticut to Kansas, where the issue of slavery was particularly bitter, believed he heard a divine call. He raided the arsenal at Harper's Ferry, Virginia, in order to arm the slaves.

In the South, men quietly stocked crates of muskets in church basements and began drilling secretly.

As the 1850's drew to a close, the clamor for secession rose louder and louder.

The drawing rooms of Dixie and the shops of New England rang with the voices of wrath. Sectional passions were building toward a new sound, terrible and unforgettable.

It was the sound of America splitting in two. . . .

Edmund Ruffin
Temporary Private, Confederate States of America

1

THE FIRST SHOT

THERE was going to be a hanging. John Brown, the antislavery crusader, had been found guilty of treason by a jury of Virginians and was under sentence to die December 2, 1859.

When the news reached Edmund Ruffin, he hastened up to Charles Town, Virginia, where the gallows was being erected. He wanted to be on the spot should the abolitionists try to rescue Brown. An attempt would be the "immediate cause of separation of Southern and Northern states," he proclaimed hopefully.

During the next few days Ruffin enlivened the streets of Charles Town. His shoulder-length white hair, his papery frailness, and the bright zeal of his eye caused people to gather and listen.

Edmund Ruffin had a lot to say—all of it about secession. He talked secession on the streets, in the parlors, and in public places. He got hold of a pike of

John Brown's, affixed a label, and paraded it for all to see: "Sample of the favors designed for us by our Northern brethren." To emphasize his point, he purchased more pikes and sent one to every governor in Dixie.

The people heard him out respectfully. Edmund Ruffin was the most distinguished agriculture scientist in the South.

Ruffin had been a leader and independent thinker since his youth. Born into Virginia's plantation aristocracy, he had not been content to leave the work to overseers and slaves. Testing and experimenting, he had made crops flourish in land played out by one hundred years of single-crop cultivation.

For forty years he had lectured and written on crop rotation, drainage, good plowing, and, above all, fertilizing with marl, a clay and lime carbonate mixture.

"You have done more good to the country than all our political men put together," he was told by former President John Tyler.

As the antislavery movement grew in the North, Ruffin determined to save the institutions of the South as he had saved its soil. He spoke and wrote profusely. In 1858 he helped found the League of United Southerners. The organization never outgrew a few local chapters; the South was not yet awakened to the danger of "Northern aggression."

Then in October, 1859, John Brown was captured as he raided the Federal arsenal at Harper's Ferry. The man who wanted to free the slaves had needed guns and ammunition. The attack was welcome propaganda to the proslavery fighter, Edmund Ruffin.

"It's exactly the incident to stir the sluggish blood of the South!" he rejoiced.

&

THE DAY of the hanging arrived. No Northern bands had showed up to rescue Brown. So Ruffin took himself early to the gallows. In order to be close, he wheedled a place among the cadets of the Virginia Military Institute. His white mane flapping at his shoulders, he kept perfect step as the boys formed behind their professor of military tactics, Major Thomas J. Jackson.

John Brown lived his last moments calmly. Ruffin beheld the other side of the coin—a Yankee as dedicated as himself.

By 1860 the South had flamed to secession. Ruffin poured on fuel. He stepped up his writing and speechmaking. In his *Slavery and Free Labor Described and Compared*, he argued that the real slaves were the Northern factory workers. In the name of home defense, he organized young ladies' shooting clubs.

His great day came in 1861. The hotheads of South Carolina proposed to fire on Fort Sumter in Charleston Harbor if the Federal garrison refused to surrender. The old man packed up and sped for the scene of action.

He kept one ear to the rumor mill. On April 9 he boarded a boat for Morris Island. The word was out: the Iron Battery on the island was to open the bombardment if the Yankees did not get out of Fort Sumter.

As Ruffin hopped off the boat he received a rousing cheer from the Palmetto Guards. In the mint-new Confederacy, the pioneer secessionist was a first citizen. The officers made him a member of the unit and asked him to discharge the first cannon.

"I shall be delighted to perform the service," Ruffin replied proudly.

At approximately 4:30 A.M., April 12, 1861, Ruffin watched a signal shell fired from Fort Johnson explode above Fort Sumter. Immediately he yanked the lanyard of an eight-inch columbiad. *The shell struck the fort at the northeast angle of the parapet*, he wrote happily in his diary.

War between the States had begun. Ruffin was hailed as a hero. He toured the South as the very soul of patriotism and the symbol of independence. Secretly, he longed to be a *fighting* hero.

That summer, as the First Battle of Manassas (Bull Run) shaped up, he rejoined the Palmetto Guards as a temporary private. According to eyewitnesses, he fired the shot that turned the Union withdrawal into a wild flight.

The Yankees had come to the Club Run bridge, jamming the road with "artillery, trains, baggage wagons, and ambulances." As the first wagon in the retreat drove onto the bridge, Ruffin fired. The buckshot struck the lead horses. They reared, upsetting the wagon so that it blocked the road.

"The whole mess of fugitives," recalled Ruffin, "escaped on foot as quickly as possible. Thus all the wagons and artillery were abandoned and everything else left by the terrified fugitives."

The war did not end with the Yankee defeat as Ruffin expected. Year after year the two armies destroyed each other with harder blows. Deafened by artillery at Manassas, Ruffin never shouldered a musket again. He devoted himself to cheering the troops.

When the war ended, the old patriot had little left. He was seventy, deaf, and shaken with palsy. Almost all of his money had been donated to the Confederacy. His home at Coggin's Point was a charred shell. Only three of his eleven children lived.

In the days of his strength he had revived the soil of his beloved Virginia. That same land he had ironically started toward ruin at Fort Sumter.

He had one more shot to fire. First, though, a final entry in his diary.

With what will be near my last breath, I hereby repeat . . . my unmitigated hatred to Yankee rule . . . and the vile Yankee race.

Edmund Ruffin closed his diary. He raised a pistol to his temple and pulled the trigger.

❧❧❧•❧❧❧

EDMUND RUFFIN

> BORN: Prince George County, Virginia, January 5, 1794.
> DIED: Amelia County, Virginia, June 18, 1865.

THE ILLUSTRATION, PAGE 13: *The Federal Arsenal at Harper's Ferry, and John Brown's pike.*

Ulysses Simpson Grant
Lieutenant General, United States of America.

2

THE CALL TO ARMS

A GAVEL rapped. A voice called, "I nominate Captain Ulysses S. Grant for chairman!"

Prior to that instant, no one in Galena had paid much notice to Grant.

The year before, he had arrived in town to take a clerkship in his father's leather store. It was generally understood he had once been a captain in the Regular Army. So the politicians thought him just the man to preside at the recruiting meeting.

Grant heard his name carried. Bash-

fully, he made his way to the front of the packed courtroom. After some prompting, he managed to state the object of the meeting.

"President Lincoln has called for seventy-five thousand men to volunteer for ninety days," he said. "The quota for Illinois is six regiments. The city of Galena ought to raise a company."

The simple direct statement was pure Grant. Others supplied the patriotic speeches, the flowery details. U. S. Grant always got to things on a straight line.

Men were eager to enlist, for the war was but three days old. When it came time to elect officers, several recruits wanted Grant to run for company commander.

"I don't know," he answered thoughtfully. "I've been a captain in the Regular Army, and I don't know as I ought to take the captaincy of volunteers."

The recruits believed he meant what he said. They elected August L. Chetlain, a wholesale grocer and the first man to volunteer.

Grant stood quietly to one side. To anyone who bothered to inquire, he promised to help in every way he could.

Afterward, he walked home alone, a figure of medium height, trudging along with shoulders slightly bent. He opened his faded blue Army coat to the April air. Six years ago, he had vowed to make the coat last ten years. With a war on, it looked suddenly as if he might have to borrow to buy a new one.

At the Milwaukee Block—the finest business building in Galena—he lit his pipe. He flipped the match in the direction of a window containing harnesses, shoepegs, awls, and hides.

"Good-by," he whispered.

Never again would he walk out that door to collect bills, or stand by the counter wrapping packages. He didn't like the work much, but he had been glad to get the job with his two up-and-coming younger brothers. Since quitting the army, he had failed at farming and real estate. The past year was his best so far. His one-third share of the firm of J. R. Grant amounted to eight hundred dollars.

He walked on, strolling westward to that part of town known as Cemetery Hill. The headstones of the graves on the summit clustered within a few yards of the back door of the small brick house at 121 High Street. Grant rented the dwelling for a hundred dollars a year.

His wife Julie and the children were asleep. He hung up his army overcoat and walked to the roll-top desk in the parlor. Only he knew the real reason he had declined to run for captain. In his boyhood, his chums had twisted Ulysses into Useless. Useless Grant! It was a prediction coming true. He had not believed those recruits would elect a failure.

Yet he felt obliged to offer his services in the war. He had been educated at West Point at government expense. He owed something in return.

He began a draft of a letter to the Governor of Illinois. "In view of my present age of thirty-nine, and my nine years service," he wrote, "I feel myself competent to command a regiment, if you see fit to intrust one to me."

The words blurred before his tired eyes. He put the letter aside, expecting to finish it the next day.

He did not go near the desk again. The next day and for the next week he was in hourly demand.

The women of Galena wished to outfit the volunteer company, known as the Jo Daviess Guards. Grant advised them on the uniform for infantry.

The wagon drivers, farmers, and clerks had to be snapped into shape in a hurry. Grant drilled them by the squads and as a unit.

Captain Chetlain and Lieutenants Campbell and Dixon were grass green; Grant taught them their duties.

It was a week of answering questions, advising, doing, and of feeling alive and needed. It was the best week in the six years since he had resigned under pressure from the army for drinking.

He was a soldier again, and respected. If only the company were cavalry instead of infantry! He would *really* show them something! At the Point he had been the best horseman in his class, better than the cavalry instructors.

For a week he was truly Captain Grant. In his clear commands and moplike thoroughness he hinted at what was to come. He never was any good at breaking down little problems. When he sold Russian bristles worth twelve cents a pound by the ounce, he usually mischarged the customer.

But when it came to seeing tremendous problems and fixing his mind on what was the true objective—when it came to that, Grant beat the world.

In a week the Jo Daviess Guards were ready to start for the state capital. Grant accompanied them. He had promised to see them through their official entry into the army.

All of Galena's fourteen thousand citizens turned out to bid their heroes farewell. Pretty girls planted bouquets in gun barrels. Men waved flags. Mothers sobbed. Sweethearts blew kisses.

Down Main Street swung the parade, blaring and blustering. In the line of march were the important people: Mayor Robert Brand, the many civic leaders, Masons, Odd Fellows, fire companies, and a brass band.

Captain Chetlain strutted at the head of his eighty men. The company crossed the bridge and boarded the train for Springfield. Behind walked

U. S. Grant, a slouch hat on his head, a pipe clamped in his mouth, a carpet-bag banging against his right thigh.

The Reverend John Vincent clambered onto the roof of a boxcar and delivered the parting address and prayer. Mayor Brand presented the color bearer with a shiny pistol.

The last aboard the train was U. S. Grant, the shabby exclerk. In three years he would command all the armies of the North and smash the Confederacy. He also would be twice elected President of the United States.

The engine puffed. The whistle screamed. The wheels turned. The noisy, flushed young men of the Jo Daviess Guards leaned out the windows of the train carrying them into oblivion. U. S. Grant sat quietly, chewing on his pipe and wondering if he would be given a colonelcy by the governor.

❧❧❧ • ❧❧❧

ULYSSES SIMPSON GRANT

> BORN: Point Pleasant, Ohio, April 27, 1822.
> DIED: Mount McGregor, New York, July 23, 1885.

THE ILLUSTRATION, PAGE 17: *General Grant's baggage wagon, with the Union Flag.*

Pierre Gustave Toutant Beauregard
General, Confederate States of America

3

THE LITTLE NAPOLEON

PIERRE GUSTAVE TOU-
TANT BEAUREGARD was
among the better pupils at the French
School in New York City. He studied
hard, earned good grades, and learned
to speak English. What interested him
most, however, was not the class work,
but the tales of war.

The school was run by two brothers
named Peugnet, who had been officers
in Napoleon's army. They reveled in
telling stories of their experiences.
Eleven-year-old Pierre listened raptly.

He began to read all about France's
military genius. What books were not
in the school library he borrowed directly from the Peugnets.

Napoleon became his idol. To be a
great soldier was his dream. For the
greater part of his life Pierre was to
shape himself after the grand master of
warfare. Nothing pleased him more
than to be called the "little Napoleon."

One morning, while vacationing at
his plantation home, Contreras, in Louisiana, he announced his wish to be a

soldier. His family protested. The Tou-tant-Beauregards were Creoles, French-men who pridefully retained Old World customs in the New. Had not they sent him to New York City to be educated? Creole boys customarily went to school in New Orleans or France. New York City was enough Americanizing!

Pierre did not retreat. Once he made up his mind that he was right, nothing could alter him. So in due time he was enrolled at the U.S. Military Academy.

He registered as Pierre Gustave Tou-tant Beauregard, dropping the hyphen. Later he was to slice off Pierre in sign-ing orders. His original name, he feared, made him sound too foreign.

At the Academy Pierre did well, as might be expected of a youth modeling himself after Napoleon. He graduated second in his class and excelled at sports and riding. He was assigned to the en-gineers, the choice branch of the army.

America was at peace. Lieutenant Beauregard was employed in strength-ening fortifications, mainly in Louisi-ana. He fretted, yearning for action. In 1846, the door to military glory finally swung open. Mexico and America de-clared war. Beauregard joined the staff of the commanding general, Winfield Scott.

His conduct in Mexico set the pat-tern for later years. Under fire, he was courageous. Afterward, he chafed be-cause he did not receive enough praise.

Following the Mexican War, he re-turned to repairing forts. When the Union split, Captain Beauregard had just been named Superintendent at West Point. He resigned and was ap-pointed brigadier general in the Con-federate Army.

❧

THE FIRST SHOT had not yet sounded when President Davis put Beauregard in command of the forces around Charleston, South Carolina. The harbor at Charleston was guarded by a system of installations. All were held by the South except Fort Sumter, which was situated on a shoal in midwater.

To capture Sumter would require neither brilliance nor daring, for it was weakly garrisoned. Even so, the man who conquered Sumter would be a hero to the people of the young Con-federacy.

Into this desirable state of affairs stepped Pierre Gustave Toutant Beau-regard. His name had an imposing ring. To many persons he seemed like Na-poleon dressed in a Confederate uni-form. He found this opinion extremely agreeable and did everything to further the impression.

He was now forty-three, short, olive-skinned, and spruce. A valet daily trimmed his black hair and mustache. The upper class of Charleston prized breeding and tradition, and into their society Beauregard, with his plantation background, blended nobly.

How fine to walk the streets and be admired! How luxurious were the dinners and fêtes in his honor. His staff of volunteer aides glittered with former governors and senators. His office was bedecked with vases of flowers, tributes from the ladies. Without a shot having been fired, he already had a reputation no man could live up to.

It was all very well mannered, those first weeks of secession. Beauregard learned that the Union officers at Fort Sumter were running low on cigars and liquor. He sent them a handsome supply of both.

Despite these pleasantries, he buckled down to organizing his command. If the Federal government in Washington refused to quit Fort Sumter, he was prepared to open fire.

Or nearly prepared. Everything was so new. He had only one rifled gun which might pierce the brick and masonry fort. The rest were old smooth-bores, which would merely chip at the walls. As for the defenders, all their guns were smoothbores which could not reach the Confederate works effectively.

When peace talks failed, orders came from President Davis to reduce Fort Sumter. The Northern stronghold could not be allowed to exist within the boundaries of the Confederacy.

In the early morning darkness of April 12, 1861, the first shell exploded above the fort. By nightfall twenty-five hundred rounds of ball and shell had poured into Sumter. The next afternoon, the fort's commander, Major Robert Anderson, ran up the white flag.

Wild cheering broke from the spectators crowded on Charleston's famous Battery. They were sure they had witnessed the end of a bloody slaughter.

Instead, they had witnessed the start. The day and a half bombardment had not killed a man, but it had exploded every hope for a peaceful secession. When the first shot had arched into the night sky, the South began to win a fort and lose a war.

Overnight Beauregard became the Confederacy's first national hero. From that peak, his popularity could only decline. Although he held important posts throughout the war, the weeks after

Fort Sumter saw him at his greatest popularity.

In combat, he had one grave failing, which, perhaps, stemmed from his early reading about Napoleon. He saw battles whole, as though remembering from a book. He adapted poorly to the sudden changes of the field.

And he adapted "poorly" to peace, prospering in railroads and lotteries. The postwar South did not want as a hero a man who refused to mourn for its shattered past. As if by general consent, he was tumbled from his place of honor beside men like Lee and Jackson.

What the people of his lifetime did not understand was how far P. G. T. Beauregard had traveled. From the Creole boy who could not speak English at school he rose to be, briefly, the hero of the Confederacy. With the peace he did not stop Americanizing himself.

He turned his face to the future—American commerce—and his back upon Napoleon.

PIERRE GUSTAVE TOUTANT BEAUREGARD

BORN: St. Bernard Parish, Louisiana, May 28, 1818.
DIED: New Orleans, Louisiana, February 20, 1893.

THE ILLUSTRATION, PAGE 21: *Fort Sumter in Charleston Harbor.*

Sally Louisa Tompkins
Captain, Confederate States of America

4

CAPTAIN SALLY

RICHMOND lay swollen with suffering. All day the huge vans of the Southern Express Company brought in load after load of bloody, pain-wracked Confederate soldiers.

The first battle of Manassas (Bull Run) was over. In place of a victory parade, gray-clad men tottered down the streets. Many lay helpless on stretchers.

The city boasted enough medical space to minister to its normal population of thirty-seven thousand. But here, overnight, was a whole new population to be cared for!

The Confederacy was as yet without a system of military hospitals. So the people opened their doors. The wounded lay in halls, on verandas, in drawing rooms. They lay in carts and in warehouses.

Among the civilians who witnessed the scenes of anguish was Sally Tompkins, a small, spirited young woman of twenty-eight. Born of a wealthy family, Sally might have boarded a steamer at Cape Fear River and traveled to Europe to escape such sights. Instead, she had decided to remain in Richmond to help as she could.

In the tortured, frightened faces of the soldiers, she saw how she could help.

That evening she sent a letter to Judge John Robertson, asking permission to use his large town house at the corner of Third and Main Streets. He replied that he intended to live in the country indefinitely. The house was hers.

Without experience, but with boundless determination and energy, the young woman transformed the home into a hospital. She equipped it out of her own pocket and recruited the first volunteers. She commandeered her mother's cook and borrowed another to tend the kitchen. She got the government to assign six surgeons as the medical staff.

Ten days after First Manassas, on July 31, 1861, Sally stood in the doorway of the building she called the Robertson Hospital and admitted the first soldier patients.

In the beginning an overflow of volunteers existed. There were more hands than work. Many a soldier got his face washed a dozen times a day by patriotic ladies eager to do something.

Women from every walk of life worked for Sally Tompkins. Those upset by the hospital's sights and odors rolled bandages at home. Others brought their servants to handle the less appealing tasks. Somehow, Sally always found women to apply bandages, fetch water, bathe the helpless, and fan flies.

Despite the help, Sally never rested. Tirelessly she moved from bed to bed. A medicine chest fastened to her side, a Bible in her hand, she was a beloved sight to "her boys."

In days when little was known of germs, she insisted upon absolute cleanliness. And not only did she run the hospital, but she obtained food besides, paying for it herself or with donations.

As the months wore on, it became increasingly difficult to procure medicine and medical instruments. Stocks captured from the more plentifully supplied North aided greatly. When medicine was later declared contraband by the North, blockade runners brought the badly needed articles from Europe, paying with cotton on the return trip. From Northern cities came Southern ladies who wore quilted petticoats that concealed quinine and morphia.

No matter how severe the shortages, Sally somehow managed to get what was needed.

26

Above the problem of supply, she faced a constant tide of resentment. Many Southerners opposed "females" in hospitals. So strong was the feeling that one of Sally's admirers angrily declared:

"There is scarcely a day passes that I do not hear some wicked remarks about the ladies who are in the hospitals, until I think, if there is any credit due them at all, it is for the moral courage they have in braving public opinion!"

One day Sally beheld a corps of ambulances drawn up at the hospital door. The officer in charge explained: a government order had discontinued the use of private hospitals for soldiers.

"I'm sorry, ma'am," he said. "All your patients will have to be removed to the new military hospitals."

Sally flew into a fury. Take her boys from their beds? She donned cape and bonnet, snatched up the hospital ledger, and marched off to see the President.

There was nothing to be done, Jefferson Davis told her kindly. The Congress had passed the law. Soldiers could be treated only at hospitals supervised by an officer with at least the rank of captain.

Sally opened the ledger. It showed there were fewer deaths in the Robertson Hospital than in any other in Richmond. Further, her hospital had returned the greatest number of men to the field.

President Davis pointed out that the military had no control over private institutions. Among other abuses, the fees charged by private hospitals were outlandishly high.

"I do not charge my patients," Sally answered. "Mercy asks no payment."

Jefferson Davis studied this frail young woman. He saw narrow eyes and hair parted down the middle and drawn sternly back to reveal her ears. No beauty, certainly. But a woman of marvelous dignity and force.

He pondered a way out. If she could operate the hospital as part of the army . . . there!

On September 9, 1861, Sally Tompkins was commissioned a captain of cavalry, unassigned. She was the first and only woman to become an officer of the Confederate Army. She accepted the commission, though refusing the pay.

And her boys stayed in their beds. Indeed, the hospital continued to receive the wounded until April 2, 1865. The more serious cases were kept under treatment until June 13, when the last soldier was strong enough to be moved.

Throughout the conflict the Robertson Hospital had accepted 1,333 wounded men. The death rate—seventy-three men—was exceptionally low.

After the war "Captain Sally" turned down numerous offers of marriage from former officers and soldiers. She retained, however, an active interest in veterans' groups.

In her last years her small funds gave out, and she went to live in the Home for Confederate Women, in Richmond. Although old and impoverished, she was not forgotten.

Two chapters of the United Daughters of the Confederacy were formed in her name. The R. E. Lee Camp, Confederate Veterans, made her an honorary member.

At the age of eighty-three, the lone woman officer of the Confederate Army died in Richmond. She was laid to rest with full military honors.

SALLY LOUISA TOMPKINS

BORN: Poplar Grove, Virginia, November 9, 1833.
DIED: Richmond, Virginia, July 25, 1916.

THE ILLUSTRATION, PAGE 25: *A Confederate field ambulance.*

Thaddeus Sobieski Coulincourt Lowe
Balloonist

5

FATHER OF THE AIR FORCE

WERE the Confederates going to attack Washington? The question plagued General Irvin McDowell, the Union commander. Reports brought in by his scouts were confusing, incomplete.

The defeat at Bull Run (Manassas) had sent panic streaking through the North. Washington was without defense. Two days after the war's first major battle, McDowell's army of three-month volunteers was still a beaten and demoralized mob. Clerks and factory hands had not yet recovered from the shock of blood and bullets.

McDowell wanted information that was clear and whole. What about the young aeronaut, Thaddeus Lowe? He had been pleading for a chance to act as an observer in his balloon. There was logic in his reasoning. High in the air, a scout could see a hundred times farther than on foot, where vision was bounded by the nearest tree, hillock, or enemy patrol.

Veteran soldiers contemptuously viewed balloons as sideshow attractions. McDowell's own doubts were strong. But his need for information was stronger. He ordered Thaddeus Lowe to fly over the enemy's lines and find out what was going on.

For days Lowe had kept everything in readiness, hoping for this chance. His balloon, the *Enterprise,* was inflated with gas and lurching at its tethers. He bade his young wife, Leontine, farewell, climbed into the basket, cast free, and began to ascend. If everything went right, he would be back on the ground before dark.

But in order to pass over the enemy, he had to drift westward, and the west-flowing air current was low. Until he had gained an altitude beyond the range of Confederate guns, he was in constant peril.

Slowly Lowe drifted above the Warrenton Turnpike to Stone Bridge. He was now between opposing lines. He floated directly over Bull Run creek. Below him the Southerners had outlasted and routed the Northerners three days before.

The land was scarred white. He sailed over a hill bearing the ruins of two farmhouses, Stone House and Henry House. There the fighting had been fiercest, and dead horses and broken wagons lay scattered still. Beyond the houses he saw where one Union force—Colonel William T. Sherman's brigade—had stood firmly while the Yankees were fleeing everywhere along the line.

The balloon passed into Confederate territory. Gray patrols rode under him, pointing and staring in disbelief. None menaced him. The horsemen regarded him more with curiosity than hostility.

Lowe surveyed the Confederate positions. He saw nothing to confirm General McDowell's fears: no supply trains, no massing of troops. The Confederates did not intend to attack Washington!

He rose to catch an easterly air stream back to Union lines. General McDowell was at Arlington and Lowe planned to land there and make his report. But as he neared friendly ground, a bullet whistled by his left ear.

His own men were firing at him! Descending, he heard shouts. What was it—they wanted him to show his flag? He had not thought to bring one. Vainly he tried to assure the soldiers that he was not a Confederate spy.

⊷

MEANWHILE the wind had changed and was pushing him west again. Lowe resigned himself to landing between lines. Toward twilight three hills reared directly in his path. He had released so much gas in attempting to land that he was unable to clear the hills. He started down, aiming at a group of trees that might screen him from unfriendly pickets.

The basket lodged in branches ten feet above the ground. Lowe injured his ankle jumping down. Otherwise, he was unharmed, and apparently unseen.

He judged the Union lines were two miles away—too far a hike on a painful ankle. Besides, he did not care to leave his equipment for the Confederates.

He freed the balloon, deflated it, and packed it and the ropes inside the basket. When he had finished, night had fallen. Wearily he pillowed his head on the varnished India silk of the gas bag and dozed off.

The man who so calmly closed his eyes in enemy territory had learned early to fend for himself. Although but twenty-nine and self-educated, Lowe had already perfected several aeronautic methods and instruments. For the past seven years he had earned his livelihood mainly as a circus balloonist, taking up passengers for a fare: a dollar in a captive balloon, five dollars for a free flight.

He had planned to fly across the Atlantic Ocean and had built the biggest balloon in history, the *Great Western*. While on a practice run across country, he had landed to refuel in South Caro-

lina. There he had rudely learned war had broken out between the states. Seized and nearly shot as a spy, he had been saved by the timely arrival of a local admirer. Afterwards, he always maintained he was "the first prisoner of war."

He might be the first prisoner to be captured twice, he thought, awakening to the crunch of footsteps. Fortunately, it was a squad of four Union soldiers. They had been directed to the spot by Lowe's wife. Leontine had rightly estimated where her husband would come to earth!

Lowe refused to leave the *Enterprise*, which was his own property. The soldiers departed. At daybreak, Leontine arrived, disguised as an old farm woman. She brought an ancient horse and wagon. Lowe and his balloon were hidden under a tarpaulin.

Confederate pickets did not notice anything suspicious in the slim, humped figure in a shapeless dress and raglike shawl. Leontine slipped unchallenged into Federal lines with her precious cargo.

In spite of his swollen ankle, Lowe proceeded directly to Arlington House and reported to General McDowell. The general was elated to learn the enemy was not gathering. Immediately he rushed the good news to Washington by telegraph.

Lowe's flight had done more than relieve official minds of the worry of attack. It had proved balloons were not merely carnival attractions. They could vastly increase the scope and speed of reconnaissance, and therefore had great military value.

President Lincoln saw to it that Professor Thaddeus Lowe was appointed to the new office of Chief of Aeronautics, United States Army. Lowe was intrusted with organizing a corps of five observation balloons.

Thaddeus Lowe fulfilled the faith of Abraham Lincoln. From his five balloons grew the United States Air Force.

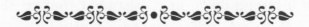

THADDEUS SOBIESKI COULINCOURT LOWE

> BORN: Jefferson Mills, New Hampshire, August 20, 1832.
> DIED: Pasadena, California, January 16, 1913.

THE ILLUSTRATION, PAGE 29: *Lowe's balloon "Intrepid" over the battlefield.*

Jefferson Davis
President, Confederate States of America

6

THE LOST CAUSE

ON a balmy May morning a strikingly handsome man left his suite at the Spotswood Hotel in Richmond, Virginia, and started for his office in the Customs House. On the way he found many objects to admire, and one to ponder.

He walked "straight as an Indian chief." Born in a log cabin, he was a West Point graduate and a self-made aristocrat. He had been a combat hero in Mexico, a United States Congressman, a Senator, Secretary of War, and

a planter. He was Jefferson Davis, unanimously elected President of the Confederate States of America.

The nation was three months old on this, his second official day in the new capital. He enjoyed looking at the neat white houses and stately church spires, the green lawns of Capitol Square, and the statues of George Washington.

But it was not upon these pleasing sights that his deep-set gray eyes lingered meditatively. It was upon the Tredegar Iron Works.

The ugly, enormous, slate-roofed structure rose by the James River. Inside those smoky walls was Dixie's only rolling mill of any consequence, the one foundry in the entire South equipped to cast cannon.

Big as it was, Davis knew it was not big enough. He must depend on cotton-needy Europe to arm his nation of farmers. An outflow of Southern cotton for an inflow of European munitions.

In time new factories would share production with the Tredegar Iron Works. A congress and a cabinet would share the duties of government with Jefferson Davis. Yet through four years of war, one mill and one man would carry most of the burden.

The Confederacy was founded on the principle of states' rights: the individual states must be safeguarded from the might of the national government. As President, Davis supported an opposite program. The interests of any single state he sacrificed to the whole.

Champions of states' rights leaped for his throat. They formed a bitter anti-Davis party. The most influential Southern newspapers joined the ranks against the President and strong central control. Their pages offered the opposition a loud and relentless voice.

High-strung and touchy, Jefferson Davis refused to give an inch. He hated criticism and even regarded sincere disagreement as a personal insult. Too frequently he did not tell his political foes his reasons for certain actions.

His mind admitted of only two kinds of Confederates—friend and enemy. Once classified, a man could expect the best or the worst, regardless of ability. Mediocre Braxton Bragg was pampered; Joseph Johnston was abused.

Self-seeking politicians knew him as incorruptible. They used him to win favor with the voters back home. They approved bills with local bias, relying upon Davis's veto to avoid national harm.

The North's hatred of slavery baffled him. He had always treated his slaves generously. He saw to it that they were happy and well cared for. His own experience showed that slavery was a blessing to the Negro race, not an evil. Why must the Yankees seek to force their beliefs upon the South?

"All we ask is to be let alone," he had declared in his first message to the Confederate Congress. In vain had he negotiated with the Union to withdraw from military posts in the South.

BRILLIANT, sensitive, and honest, Davis tried to run the new government by himself. For his Cabinet he chose undistinguished men, with the exception of Judah Benjamin, the master of all trades. To a lesser degree, he tried to run the army via his constitutional rank of commander in chief.

He had accepted the Presidency with regret. The position he wanted was commander of the armies in the field. Seven years in the Regular Army had instilled in him an exaggerated opinion of his military prowess.

He believed himself the equal of his best generals. Upon none did he bestow complete authority until the very end. Only in Robert E. Lee did he recognize a military mind on a plane with his own.

When the Union tightened its stranglehold, he still cherished the image of himself as a warrior. "If I could take one wing and Lee the other," he confided to his wife, "I think we could between us wrest a victory from them."

By then there were to be no more victories. For Jefferson Davis there was only the worsening of the neuralgia that nearly robbed him of his eyesight. Down by the James the great Tredegar Iron Works stood like a starving hulk. Inferior materials resulted in second-rate cannon. Shortages of parts hobbled another piece of machinery each day.

A cup of coffee sold for three dollars and a potato for one dollar. Hope was draining. A favorite tune was "When This Cruel War Is Over." Colonies of wealthy Southerners were springing up in London and Paris.

Richmond fell. Lee surrendered at Appomattox.

Davis made his decision. Holding to the vision of Southern independence, he set up his capital by the roadside. With him traveled his Cabinet, the Treasury gold, and a cavalry escort.

He intended to join General E. Kirby Smith of the Trans-Mississippi Department and continue the fight. While he was on the move, the Confederacy dissolved. The midnight of his brave young government had come.

He pushed southward, hoping to get out of the country. Federal cavalry overtook him on May 10, 1865, in a pine forest near Irwinville, Georgia. Under arrest, he was transported in a closed ambulance, manacled hand and foot like a murderer, jeered at and reviled.

For two years he was held as a state prisoner in Fort Monroe, Virginia. He was released on May 13, 1867, without ever having been brought to trial.

A free man, he traveled to Europe, served as president of an insurance company, and eventually retired to Belvoir, the home of a friend in Mississippi.

He had fought the industrial giant of the North and held it off for four years. No man could have done more.

"Had a man less sober-minded and less strong than Davis been in his place," said a Southern statesman, "the Confederacy would not have gone down in material ruin—it would have been buried in disgrace."

Jefferson Davis lived twenty-seven years after having voiced the one great hope of all Southerners: *"All we want is to be left alone."*

JEFFERSON DAVIS

> BORN: Christian County, Kentucky, June 3, 1808.
> DIED: New Orleans, Louisiana, December 6, 1889.

THE ILLUSTRATION, PAGE 33: *The Confederate Capitol at Richmond.*

The _Merrimack_ and the _Monitor_

7

VALIANT MAKESHIFT

AT THE outset of the war the North destroyed every United States military base in the South that could not be defended. Arsenals, supply depots, and Navy yards were hurriedly demolished lest they fall into enemy hands. War vessels were scuttled when their Southern deckhands balked at sailing North.

One of the scuttled ships was a thirty-five-hundred-ton steam frigate, _Merrimack_. For two months she rested in the river mud off Portsmouth, Virginia. Then one day in June, 1861, she was raised from the grave. The North, which had forgotten her, began to get alarming reports of a monstrous rebirth.

The Confederates had cut her down to the berth deck and were encasing her in an iron shell to the water line. When completed, rumor had it, she would crush the wooden ships of Union fleets like eggshells. She would tear open the blockade, level Washington, and put New York and all the cities of the Atlantic coast under tribute. Nothing would be able to resist her! Nothing, that is, except another like her.

Gideon Welles, Lincoln's Secretary of the Navy, frantically advertised for plans for "ironclad steam batteries." John Ericsson, a Swedish-born engineer and inventor, submitted the winning design. On October 23, the keel of his craft was laid at Greenpoint, New York.

In the shipyards was waged the race to control the rivers and harbors. The North relied upon vastly superior facilities, the South on its four-month head start.

The South won by a day.

On March 5, 1862, the *Merrimack* was launched at Norfolk, Virginia. (Although rechristened *Virginia*, she continued to be known by her old name.) Had Gideon Welles seen her, he would have refused to believe this was the demon he feared. Men who did see her bet that she would sink like a stone.

She did not sink, though she did behave distressingly like a stone. Her worn-out engines were capable of five knots only. It required half an hour to turn her. Nevertheless, considering the shortages of time and material, her builder, John L. Porter, had done a formidable job.

On March 8 the patched-together ironclad inched down the Elizabeth River. Anchored off Newport News in Hampton Roads were several wooden ships of the Union blockading fleet, headed by the fifty-gun frigate *Congress* and the thirty-gun sloop *Cumberland*. The *Merrimack* wallowed toward them like a huge turtle. At 2:00 P.M. she started to snap.

The *Congress* was raked with a starboard broadside. Plowing on, the ironclad rammed into the *Cumberland*, opening a hole under the fore rigging. Both Union ships continued to fire uselessly at their squat tormentor.

At 3:30 P.M. the stately *Cumberland* sank. An hour later the proud *Congress*, aground and helpless, surrendered. Three more Union ships bravely attempted to enter the battle. They too ran aground. The *Minnesota*, sister ship of the original *Merrimack*, was close enough to employ her guns. Because of the shallow water, the ironclad could not reach her. It was late afternoon. The Confederates retired to Sewell's Point, postponing the capture of the *Minnesota* until the following day.

୬

THE one-sided battle resounded around the world. The crude and clumsy *Merrimack* had demonstrated her disdain for the sleek wooden warships. A new era in naval warfare was dawning.

The *Merrimack* steamed forth at daybreak to capture the *Minnesota*. The Confederates planned to destroy her and then the rest of the Union blockading fleet, even though their ironclad was below fighting strength.

Her commander, Commodore Franklin Buchanan, had been sent to a hospital ashore, severely wounded. Twenty out of the three hundred men in the crew were casualties. Nearly everything outside the four-inch iron plating—steampipes, anchor, smokestack, and the muzzles of two guns—had been shot away. The fifteen-hundred-pound cast-iron ram, the most effective weapon, had broken off in the *Cumberland*.

As the *Merrimack* approached her victim, a small, weird-looking object snorted out from behind the *Minnesota*. The Confederates, who had heard of an ironclad being built in the North, nevertheless stared in amazement. One oarsman shouted, "A tin can on a shingle!"

It was the Northern ironclad, all right. The *Monitor*! Like the *Merrimack*, most of her was under water. And like the *Merrimack*, she seemed ready to roll over any instant. But she contained features that made her the most powerful warship afloat.

She had arrived at Hampton Roads the previous night, having been towed from New York. During the trip she had nearly foundered twice. Her crew of fifty-eight had eaten nothing but bread on the trip; most had not slept for forty-eight hours.

It was shortly before 9:00 A.M., March 9, 1862, when the untested *Monitor* advanced to meet the *Merrimack* in the first battle between ironclads.

Ship to ship, the contest was unequal. The *Merrimack* had been built to destroy the blockading wooden ships. The *Monitor* had been built to destroy the *Merrimack*. The Confederate ship, with a wooden hull and iron topsides, was the makeshift experiment of a struggling infant nation. The Union ship, truly an ironclad throughout, had rolled from the shipyards of the greatest maritime nation in the world.

The *Monitor's* two eleven-inch guns were mounted in a revolving tower (a design that revolutionized naval arms). These guns were heavier than any of the ten aboard the *Merrimack*. In addition, the Union ship, being smaller and drawing only twelve feet of water, could move anywhere. The *Merrimack*, besides being unwieldy, had a draft of twenty-two feet that restricted her to a narrow zone of combat in midstream.

Nevertheless, the valiant *Merrimack* held her own. For six hours the foes slugged and bumped each other, exchanging shots that would have demolished any wooden ship in short order.

The battle ended when the *Monitor* withdrew because of the blinding of her commander, Lieutenant John Wordon. The *Merrimack* waited for twenty minutes and then steamed away to Norfolk. When the *Monitor* returned to the scene, the *Merrimack* was departing.

The North had gained a moral victory. The blockading fleet had been saved. As long as there was the watch-dog *Monitor*, Washington, New York and all the seacoast cities were safe.

Neither government wished to risk losing its ironclad in a renewal of the battle. So the two ships never had at one another again.

On May 9, 1862, the *Merrimack* was scuttled to prevent her capture by Union forces occupying Norfolk. The *Monitor* sank in a gale off Cape Hatteras on December 13, 1862.

In the time since their duel, neither had seen decisive action. Yet shipyards all over the world were hurriedly refitting to build ironclads. At Hampton Roads the age of the wooden warship had died in smoke and clanging iron.

❧❧❧❧•❧•❧❧❧❧

THE ILLUSTRATION, PAGE 37: *Naval engagement between the "Merrimack" (left) and "Monitor" at Hampton Roads, Virginia, March 9, 1862. Northern frigate in background.*

James J. Andrews
Spy, United States of America

8

RAIDERS ON RAILS

EARLY in the morning of April 12, 1862, nineteen young men, arriving singly and in pairs, entered the room of James J. Andrews in the Marietta Hotel, Marietta, Georgia. Although dressed as civilians, the youths were in reality Yankee soldiers from Ohio regiments. They had volunteered for a "secret and dangerous mission."

Having walked straight into the heart of enemy country, they now stood assembled to receive their final instructions. Andrews, a secret service agent, gave them the details of his daring plot.

The Western Atlantic Railroad, running between Marietta and Chattanooga, Tennessee, was the principal supply route for the Confederate forces in Tennessee. If the railroad was crippled, the Confederates would be shut off from their bases long enough for Union General Ormsby Mitchel to capture Chattanooga.

Their mission, Andrews explained, was to steal a train, rip tracks, cut telegraph wires, and burn bridges between Marietta and Chattanooga, and then escape on foot. He looked at the volunteers and gave each of them a chance to back out, honorably. None did.

An hour later the squad of Yanks sauntered carelessly up to the ticket booth and bought tickets for a mail-carrying express, *The General.*

They rode as passengers for eight miles—as far as Big Shanty. Because it had no telegraph connections, Andrews had selected Big Shanty as the ideal place to seize the train.

With a long squeal, the wheels ground to a halt. W. A. Fuller, the conductor, swung down the aisle. "Big Shanty!" he hollered. "Twenty minutes for breakfast!"

Andrews saw row upon row of tents. Since his last check, the place had been turned into a Confederate Army camp!

The young raiders glanced at their chief anxiously. He rose and nodded for them to follow. They would steal the train from under the nose of a Confederate Army!

The passengers filed from the train on the right side, the raiders from the left. Andrews and Private Wilson Brown, an engineer in peacetime, went forward to make certain the switch ahead of the locomotive was open.

As several Confederate soldiers watched in growing curiosity, Andrews uncoupled a section of the train—the locomotive, tender, and three empty boxcars.

Then he signaled. In a matter of seconds, Brown, another engineer named William Knight, and Alf Wilson, a fireman, leaped into the cab. The other raiders piled into the last boxcar. Coolly Andrews waved the go-ahead.

Brown yanked the valve wide open. The wheels spun, slipping in place for a terrible moment. Finally they caught with a jerk that tumbled the men in the boxcar. *The General* chugged away, leaving Big Shanty in an uproar.

❧

THE first hurdle had been jumped. With four months of planning behind him, Andrews felt confident of success.

According to the timetable in his pocket, two trains were headed his way, down the single track. By maintaining the schedule of the captured train, Andrews could avoid a collision. Then, racing at full throttle, he could go on to the Oostenaula and Chickamauga bridges, burn them, and join General Mitchel before night.

The raiders were in high spirits. But a seemingly small matter was eventually to loom dangerously across their path. Andrews had delayed the raid twenty-four hours. The day before had been clear and dry, and all trains ran on time. Now rain fell, and the trains were off schedule.

And back at Big Shanty, Fuller, the conductor, acted to thwart the raiders. Accompanied by Anthony Murphy, a railroad man, he started in pursuit, first on foot and then by handcar.

Far ahead of them Andrews had stopped *The General*. The Yanks cut telegraph wires and loaded a boxcar with crossties, which were to be used as kindling to fire the bridges.

Farther along, wood and water were taken on. Andrews calmly told a suspicious railroad agent a story he was to repeat often: he was a Confederate officer running emergency ammunition to General Beauregard at Corinth.

The General and its captors proceeded thirty miles to Kingston. Here they waited on a sidetrack for a local freight to pass. When it arrived, it bore a red flag, meaning an extra train was following. The second train steamed by, and to Andrews' dismay, it too bore a red flag.

Through an agonizing hour of delay, Andrews kept his head. The passengers of other waiting trains began to ask questions. Andrews sent back a message to the sixteen men cooped in the boxcar: "Be ready to fight."

Fortunately, the second extra train rolled by and the raiders moved on without being discovered. After four miles they paused to uproot a length of track. Suddenly the whistle of a pursuing engine shrieked in their ears.

It was Fuller and Murphy aboard an old engine they had found back at Etowah. With a furious heave, the raiders tore loose the track.

Fuller barely prevented a wreck. Undaunted, he and Murphy quit the blocked locomotive and proceeded on foot. They flagged down *The Texas*, a troop train which had nearly given Andrews trouble. Fuller dropped the cars, got forty soldiers in the tender, and, turning about, started off in relentless pursuit.

Mile after mile flew by at breakneck speed. Several times the desperate Yanks nearly dislodged a rail. The Confederates would thunder within rifle range, and the work had to be abandoned. Another minute or two would have seen the job done, and put *The General* beyond reach.

One by one the trailing boxcars were unfastened. *The Texas* slowed, caught the cars, and pushed them to the next siding. The raiders dropped crossties and other obstacles. Miraculously, *The*

Texas managed to stay on the rails.

Then suddenly *The General* coughed, faltered, and stopped. After ninety wild miles, it had run out of fuel. Andrews and his raiders had failed to inflict any major damage. With nothing left but to save themselves, they jumped to the ground.

All were captured. Because of their civilian clothes, they were treated as spies. Andrews and seven of his men were hanged. The rest attempted to escape, and eight got away. The remaining six were returned to prison, where they stayed until they were paroled on March 17, 1863.

Almost a year after they had gathered in the hotel room in Marietta, the six exprisoners were brought to Washington as heroes. Secretary of War Stanton promised promotions to first lieutenants, and handed to each—as he would to all the surviving raiders—a morocco case.

The six gaunt men stared proudly. Inside the cases were the first Congressional Medals of Honor ever awarded.

❧❧❧•❧❧❧

JAMES J. ANDREWS

BORN: Kentucky, 1826 (?).
DIED: Atlanta, Georgia, June 7, 1862.

THE ILLUSTRATION, PAGE 41: *"The General," an engine of the Western Atlantic Railroad, captured by Andrews' Raiders.*

David Glasgow Farragut
Vice Admiral, United States of America

9

CONQUEROR OF NEW ORLEANS

"ALL HANDS!"

Hooded lanterns bobbed in the holds of the Union ships anchored on the Mississippi. Quietly quartermasters and their mates whispered at the sleeping tars, "*All hands!*"

With low grunts the men of the West Gulf Blockading Fleet dropped from their hammocks and hurried to battle. At 2:00 A.M. a pair of red lanterns was hoisted to the mizzen peak of the *Hartford*, flagship of the fleet. It was the signal to weigh anchor. In three divisions the seventeen ships started up the Mississippi.

Seventy miles upriver slept New Orleans, the Southland's biggest port and richest city. Its capture would split the Confederacy in two along the line of the river.

To reach New Orleans seemed nigh impossible. The wooden Northern ships would have to thrust past a triple layer of defenses: a barricade across the river, two forts, and the ships of the South's River Defense Fleet.

For eight days Commander David Porter had attempted to destroy the forts with his twenty mortar schooners. He had exhausted nearly all his 285-pound shells and fuses in a vain attempt.

At heart, few of the Northern officers believed their fleet could pierce the Southern defenses. Wasn't one gun on land better than three afloat? The guns of the forts outnumbered theirs without the tactical advantage. Besides, it was against naval law to pit wooden ships against stone forts.

One of the few officers who believed the fleet could get through was the man who counted most, an old salt named David Farragut.

A member of the United States Navy since he was nine, Farragut, at sixty, was realizing his lifelong ambition: a flag of command. His record had been good but, because of limited opportunity, not outstanding. A Southerner by birth, he had moved from Norfolk, Virginia, to a cottage above New York City when the war commenced. This action, in the mind of the men in Washington, showed loyalty and superior character. So the old sailor was called from semi-retirement and asked to capture New Orleans.

Now the red lanterns were up. The seventeen gunboats were cutting the Mississippi. Nothing could stay the attack. Farragut had given the order, contrary to all the rules of naval warfare. He could only climb twenty-five feet into the port mizzen rigging of the *Hartford* and "abide the outcome."

The first obstacle was the barricade of sunken ships, logs, and chains linked across the river. The night before a narrow path had been secretly opened. Could the ships find the path in the darkness?

The leading Union ship, the little gunboat *Cayuga*, pushed cautiously into the barrier—and through! The other ships left the formation and squeezed into the passage one by one.

One thousand yards above the barricade, the Confederates looked down upon the scene from two powerful forts, Jackson on the left bank, and St. Philip on the right. At 3:40 A.M. their guns opened fire.

Farragut spread his feet on the ratlines and leaned back against the shrouds. Through a pair of borrowed opera glasses, the old sailor watched the shells bursting.

The little *Cayuga*, out in front, was through the barrier and exchanging shots with Fort Jackson. The flagship *Hartford*, ninth in line, passed safely into unobstructed water. To conserve ammunition, Farragut had not yet allowed her guns to be fired.

Signal Officer B. S. Osbon begged the admiral to come down from the rigging. Reluctantly, he left his perch. Shortly afterward, a shell struck the spot where he had stood.

The ships of the first division had slipped past the forts and were engaging the Confederate gunboats. The middle of Union fleet was running the forts, and the tail was still slithering through the barricade.

The *Hartford*, heading the second division, steamed abreast of the forts. Now the gunners loaded and fired at will, pouring out grape, canister, and shrapnel. Darkness and thick smoke were broken by the thunder of guns and the slanted jets of flames. Ships bumped. The *Brooklyn*, trailing the *Hartford*, wandered from bank to bank, the captain having lost all sense of direction.

᪣

Suddenly two fire rafts came drifting toward the pack of wooden hulls. The fires lighted the battle like two huge torches. The *Hartford* dodged the two rafts, but just past the forts encountered a third.

This one she could not dodge. It was guided by the Confederate tugboat *Mosher*. The *Hartford*, in veering sharply, ran ashore. The brave men of the *Mosher* pushed under her guns and got the blazing raft alongside. In a minute flames ran the entire port side of the flagship and sped halfway up the masts.

It was Mr. Osbon who saved the day. Swiftly he rolled three twenty-pound shells across the deck, uncapped them, and nudged them overboard and into the burning raft. The resulting blast sank the raft.

As the fire crew beat the flames under control, the *Hartford* backed into deep water and proceeded upriver.

In seventy minutes, the forts had been passed. By daybreak, the Confederate fleet had been crushed. Union losses were only thirty-seven killed and one hundred and forty-seven wounded. Farragut's ship had been hit eighteen times and suffered two killed and thirty wounded.

At one o'clock the next day, April 25, 1862, the Union fleet dropped anchor before undefended New Orleans. The citizens raged, but the officials of the city surrendered. Roof-top fighting was avoided.

The North thus gained an important objective: control of the mouth of the

Mississippi. The South lost its largest port and more. The demonstration of Union seapower caused England to back off from helping the Confederates split the blockade.

The early newspaper accounts of the victory scarcely mentioned Farragut. Credit went to General Benjamin Butler, whose troops occupied the city on May 1, and to Commander Porter, who took the surrender of Forts Jackson and St. Philip on April 28. Butler and Porter were well known. Who was David Farragut?

Recognition came slowly to the old sailor. When it came, however, it swept him like a flood. On July 30, he was commissioned rear admiral, the highest rank then in the Navy. Before the war ended he was vice admiral. On July 26, 1866, the rank of admiral was especially created for him.

Like many men of fame, David Farragut mastered his profession slowly and patiently. When his great opportunity came—his first command—he was sixty years old. His deeds are the proof that the willingness to take great risks for great ends lies within the man himself, no matter what his years.

❦❦❦·❦❦❦

DAVID GLASGOW FARRAGUT

BORN: Campbell's Station, Tennessee, July 5, 1801.
DIED: Portsmouth, New Hampshire, August 14, 1870.

THE ILLUSTRATION, PAGE 45: *The Flagship "Hartford" attacked by a ram and a fire-raft in the Mississippi River.*

Thomas Jonathan Jackson
Lieutenant General, Confederate States of America

10

LEE'S RIGHT ARM

A WEATHER-BEATEN Southern officer sat on a fence outside New Market, Virginia, sucking a lemon. There was little to set him apart from the troops eating their lunch in the fields nearby.

If anything, he was shabbier. He wore a single-breasted coat, threadbare with sixteen years of use. Tilted forward on his head was a dusty flat cap. Its visor seemed about to slide down his nose as the lemon wiggled in his beard.

He was General Thomas Jackson. The fence on which he sat was, figuratively, his threshold to greatness. In a few weeks his popularity would zoom until it rivaled that of Robert E. Lee.

Nobody thought of him as Thomas Jackson. Since First Manassas (Bull Run), people called him "Stonewall." Then, as a brigade commander, he had held his position in the crises of battle. Inspired by his example, a dying general had rallied his retreating men with the cry, "Look, there is Jackson, standing like a stone wall!"

"Stonewall" Jackson it was, unto eternity.

He had other nicknames. At the Virginia Military Institute, where he'd taught just before the war, the cadets had thought him queer. They smirked at the occasional halts in his lectures. Was his mind drifting back to the Mexican War? 'Twas said he'd been a hero—breveted major eighteen months after graduating West Point. The cadets winked. Thomas? No. *"Tom Fool!"*

"Old Jack," his men named him. Soldiers had a fondness for affixing "old" to any respected commander. He was thirty-eight.

"The Lemon Squeezer," the wits called him and wondered where he got his everlasting lemons. Nobody else had seen the fruit for months.

"Crazy as a March hare!" bellowed General Dick Ewell when Jackson's secretiveness stranded him as the enemy approached. Ewell soon changed his opinion.

Men commonly underrated the plain-looking Jackson at first glimpse. "He had the appearance of being a man of not above average ability," one officer said.

The simple appearance and the stern manner stemmed from deeply rooted religious feelings. "God has blessed our arms," he would explain after a battle. Before one, he prayed. But he remained up late with his maps figuring out ways to help the Lord.

A Bible always slapped in his saddle-bag. He disliked marching on Sunday, and his men chuckled at his being forced to. For his chief of staff, he chose a preacher, a man without military experience.

In all things he was his own iron master. Once he had tasted liquor. He liked it so well he gave it up. He never revealed his plans, even to his staff, until they were ripe for execution. "If I can deceive my friends, I can make certain of deceiving my enemies."

Such was the shabby officer who sat on the fence, thoughtfully sucking a lemon. A man who seldom laughed. A man who kept his own council. A man who feared God.

He climbed to the ground, gave a last pull on his lemon, and struck the enemy in a series of thunderbolts. His little army of 17,500 performed like three times their number.

&

IN THIS, the spring of 1862, the North's General McClellan had his huge Army of the Potomac creeping up the peninsula toward Richmond. General Irwin McDowell had forty thousand guarding Washington. In the Shenandoah Valley below the Union capital, General Nathaniel Banks had twenty thousand. In the mountains of

West Virginia, General John C. Fremont had fifteen thousand. These armies had to be kept from reinforcing McClellan's hundred thousand.

Jackson hit where he was least expected. He talked like a deacon and fought like the devil. Five times he marched the length of the Valley in a campaign that has been judged flawless. He emerged as the most illustrious Confederate field commander. His infantry, traveling up to forty miles in twenty-four hours, gloried in the well-deserved title of "Jackson's foot cavalry."

From April to June he battered Banks and Fremont and thoroughly alarmed Washington. He smote with the power of fifty thousand. McDowell's forty thousand were withheld to protect the Union capital from his threat. McClellan, crying for McDowell's brigades, stalled before Richmond.

With 17,500 men and magnificent skill, Stonewall had offset the efforts of 175,000 Northern troops. Victorious, he slipped back to Richmond and helped the outnumbered Confederates repulse McClellan.

He handles his army like a whip, wrote one New York *Times* reporter. *He makes it crack in out-of-the-way corners where you scarcely thought the lash would reach.*

He acquired another nickname: "Lee's right arm." He was promoted to lieutenant general and put in command of one of the two wings of Lee's army. James Longstreet commanded the other.

Lee and Jackson operated in the absolute harmony of mind and arm. The master strategist had a master tactician. Jackson was the ideal lieutenant to carry out Lee's orders boldly and quickly. In 1862 and 1863, when the army reached its fullest prowess, they won victory after victory against superior numbers.

Although under Lee, Jackson made use of his own principles of war:

"Always mystify, mislead, and surprise the enemy if possible; and when you strike and overcome him, never let up in the pursuit so long as your men have the strength to follow; for any army routed, if hotly pursued, becomes panic-stricken and can then be destroyed by half their number.... Never fight against heavy odds, if by any possible maneuvering you can hurl your own force on only a part, and that the weakest part, of your enemy and crush it."

On May 2, 1863, at Chancellorsville, Virginia, Jackson fought his last battle. By means of one of his rapid marches, he struck the rear of the Union army under General Joseph Hooker. The enemy retreated. Jackson rode to the front to organize pursuit. Returning at dusk, he was mistaken for a Yank and tragically wounded by his own men.

Eight days later he died of pneumonia. He had lived through but half the Civil War, yet his passing left a gap that was never filled.

"I know not how to replace him," mourned Lee.

Jackson's body lay in state in Richmond, whence it was borne to Lexington, Virginia, for burial. The last words of the dying warrior lingered like a psalm:

"Let us cross over the river, and rest under the shade of the trees."

THOMAS JONATHAN JACKSON

BORN: Clarksburg, Virginia, January 21, 1824.
DIED: Guiney's Station, Virginia, May 10, 1863.

THE ILLUSTRATION, PAGE 49: *Confederate revolvers: Tucker, Sherrod & Co., "Colt", at left; Griswold & Grier "Dragoon", at right.*

1. Charleston and Savannah Railroad   2. Ashley River   3. Charleston   4. Cooper River   5. Wando River
6. Castle Pinckney   7. Fort Ripley   8. Fort Johnson (James's Island)   9. Fort Sumter   10. Fort Moultrie
11. Battery Gregg (Cummings's Point)   12. Fort Wagner
13. Sullivan's Island and Rebel Batteries

Robert Smalls
Captain, United States Transport *Planter*

11

STEAMBOAT TO FREEDOM

IT BEGAN with a joke. All the white officers had gone ashore for the night, and the Negro crewmen of the *Planter* were kidding around in the pilothouse.

A fireman put Captain Relyea's hat on Robert Smalls. Going along with the fun, Smalls folded his arms across his chest and walked with a jaunty step. His audience rocked with laughter, for Smalls looked surprisingly like the captain. Both men were short and muscular. And with the wide-brimmed straw hat pulled down over his forehead, the

Negro easily could pass for the white man—from a distance.

Smalls uncrossed his arms thoughtfully. The impersonation had tripped an exciting idea. If he had the courage, he might gain his freedom and strike a blow for the Union as well.

Robert Smalls removed the captain's hat. That same hour he started to work out a scheme for stealing the *Planter*.

The 140-foot paddle-wheel steamer was owned by one John Ferguson and chartered by the Confederacy for $125 a day. She had space for one thousand

53

soldiers and fourteen hundred bales of cotton. Because of her speed and light draft, she had become the flagship of General Rosewall Ripley, second-in-command of the defenses of Charleston, South Carolina.

Ten months earlier, Robert Smalls had signed on as a deckhand. Although a slave, he was used to hiring out; his owner, Henry McKee, always needed money. Out of his seaman's wage of sixteen dollars monthly he paid McKee fifteen. In off hours, he toiled at odd jobs to earn cash for himself.

On the night he played at being Captain Relyea, Smalls was the best wheelsman (the highest position open to a slave) in Charleston. He had saved seven hundred dollars of the eight hundred necessary to buy his family's freedom. He was twenty-three years old, a husband and a father. But white people called him "boy."

With a war on, there was only one way to freedom for him. He would deliver the *Planter* to the blockading Union fleet which lay just beyond the sand bar.

And he'd bring the Union something else—a map of the harbor's defenses. Traveling between the different Confederate forts, he had come to know their strengths and weaknesses, as well as the site of every secretly placed battery and torpedo.

⁓

ON THE EVENING of May 12, 1862, Captain Relyea and his white officers disembarked at Fort Sumter to attend a ball given by the ladies of the city. At three in the morning the ball was over, the harbor was still, and a full head of steam was in the boilers of the *Planter*.

Her Negro crew silently cut the cables and lowered them into the water by strings to avoid splashes. Smalls backed her out of Southern Wharf and started up the Cooper River.

Near the merchantman *Etowan* he dropped anchor and dispatched a rowboat to bring over the women. Twenty minutes later they were aboard—five women and three children, including Smalls' wife, Hannah, and their baby daughter, Elizabeth.

Then the *Planter* headed out to sea.

The ship steamed through the harbor as if on a routine run. Castle Pinckney slipped by. As Fort Johnson drew near, Smalls, attired in Captain Relyea's jacket and hat, tugged the rope at his shoulder. The steam whistle shrieked.

The soldiers on the fort heard the signal. If they wondered what General Ripley's flagship was about so early in the morning, they detected nothing to cause suspicion.

Smalls watched Fort Johnson and then Fort Moultrie fall behind. He felt the prick of fear. To the crew he had made everything sound so rosy and sure. What if they were discovered? Would he really have the courage to scuttle the *Planter* as he promised?

Fort Sumter appeared in the dim rays of dawn. Three miles beyond lay the ships of the Union fleet. Smalls had all he could do to keep from ordering more steam. He longed to get it over with—to spurt past Sumter and gamble on outracing its guns.

Leisurely, the ship steamed abreast of the huge island fortress. Silence gripped the deck of the *Planter*. On the parapet high above them a dozen heavy muzzles stared down. The colored men stared back. In the hold the women shushed the children.

Smalls stood by the window of the pilothouse. Captain Relyea's broad-brimmed straw hat slanted over his face. He unfolded his arms to pull the signal cord.

As the blasts died, a sentinel shouted, "Corporal of the guard! General Ripley's flagship signaling as required."

Smalls held his breath. After seconds that passed like hours, a voice called, "Let General Ripley's flagship continue."

Familiar words. Smalls had heard them often, though never with life and freedom throbbing in every syllable.

The paddles turned. The ship churned on at a steady pace. Once outside the range of the fort's guns, Smalls called for more steam.

The *Planter* jumped forward. The sudden speed-up caught the eyes of the lookouts observing her through glasses. As she passed Morris Island, the alarm flashed throughout the network of fortifications.

But the *Planter* was beyond overtaking. As she made for the Union fleet, Smalls lowered the Rebel flag. In its place he ran up a white bedsheet.

The *Onward*, nearest ship of the fleet, began turning to bring her guns to bear on the stranger. Drums beat, summoning all hands to prepare for action.

Smalls glanced up in dismay. The bedsheet hung limply from the mast. He spun the wheel, heading into the faint breeze. The white sheet fluttered into a flag of truce. The captain of the *Onward* shouted to hold fire.

Questions flew across the water. The men of the *Onward* did not trust their ears. An officer went aboard the *Planter* to investigate.

To his astonishment he received the salute of a slave standing erect and resolute in a captain's fancy jacket.

"Sir, I bring you the *Planter*, formerly the flagship of General Ripley," said Robert Smalls. "We have come to join the Union fleet."

The *Planter* became part of the fleet, and *Mister* Smalls became her captain.

His death fifty years later closed a life devoted to bettering his state and his people as a representative in the South Carolina Legislature and the United States Congress.

In 1915 white and Negro alike mourned the passing of the slave who had piloted the *Planter* on the historic trip from "boy" to man.

ROBERT SMALLS

> BORN: Beaufort, South Carolina, April 5, 1839.
> DIED: Beaufort, South Carolina, February 22, 1915.

THE ILLUSTRATION, PAGE 53: *The "Planter" with map of Charleston, S. C. Harbor.*

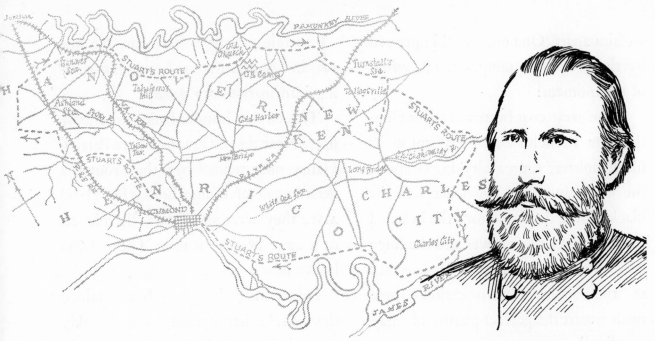

James Ewell Brown Stuart
Major General, Confederate States of America

12

THE EYES OF THE ARMY

"JEB" STUART swayed to the twanging of a banjo. At twenty-nine the leader of Lee's cavalry loved music and merriment, and both were sure to burst forth wherever he pitched his headquarters.

Bird mimics, a ventriloquist, and Negro dancers and singers outdid themselves for Jeb and his staff of handsome young men. But tonight Jeb had to strain to be merry. His thoughts drifted beyond headquarters to where he had twelve hundred picked cavalry sleeping on their weapons, awaiting his orders.

Jeb called for his favorite tune, "Jine the Cavalry." He threw back his golden-red head and sang at the top of his voice. Then he ordered everyone to an early bed.

At two the next morning—June 12, 1862—he awoke his staff. "Gentlemen," he said, "in ten minutes every man must be in his saddle."

As Jeb mounted his horse, his golden spurs glinted in the moonlight. He loved finery, and his splendid uniform set him apart. One onlooker, impressed by the gorgeous young general, wrote of the moment:

"The gray coat buttoned to his chin; the light French saber, the pistol in its black holster; the cavalry boots above the knee, and the brown hat with its black plume floating above the bearded features, the brilliant eyes and the huge mustache, which curled with laughter at the slightest provocation—these made Stuart the perfect picture of a gay cavalier."

An artillery officer called after him, "How long will you be gone?"

"It may be for years, and it may be forever," was the lighthearted answer.

Jeb and his officers joined the twelve hundred of cavalry, who were bivouacked a few miles from headquarters. The troopers were silently prodded awake and closed into a column of fours. By five o'clock, the vanguard was trotting from Richmond, pointed north.

Jeb's orders were "to make a secret movement to the rear of the enemy now posted on the Chickahominy." Particularly, General Lee wanted to know if General McClellan's right flank was vulnerable.

JEB relished the assignment. No one in either army was better at gathering information at a gallop.

The twelve hundred pierced enemy lines. Near the old tavern where Patrick Henry once tended bar, they routed a detachment of Union horse. By 11:00 A.M., they were sighted by the pickets of a large Northern unit. The column broke into a gallop.

Before much longer, Jeb ascertained that McClellan's right was weakly pegged. There were no trenches, nothing to worry an infantry assault.

Jeb had accomplished his aim, and here he might have turned back. The enemy, however, would be expecting him to retrace his steps, and would lie in ambush. The alternative was to return to Richmond by galloping ahead —by circling behind McClellan's army, a ride of nearly a hundred miles!

Jeb decided for the long way home. What followed were three days of destruction, and three days of hapless chase by a bewildered Union cavalry.

Jeb's men fell upon Union supply lines like hungry wolves. Wagons and stores were burned, transports and depots looted, telegraph wires cut, and prisoners taken. Behind him Jeb left fires that burned for hours and smoke that could be seen for miles.

Deeper and deeper Jeb slashed into Union territory. With every mile it seemed less possible that he could pull the column out. Yet every man had unwavering faith in him. A few of the veterans repeated for the benefit of the newer men Jeb's favorite rule of war:

"A cavalry can trot away from anything. A gallop is a gait unbecoming to a soldier, unless he is going toward the enemy. Remember that. We gallop toward the enemy, and trot away. Always."

Gallop toward the enemy they had. But now, going southward, going home, the raiders were too weary to trot, though pursuit was close. The column plodded toward the Chickahominy River. Once across it, Jeb felt, he was past catching.

Men went fast asleep in the saddle. General Stuart slept with one leg crooked over the pommel, his arms folded, his chin sunk on his chest. Worn and dust smeared, he looked a far cry from the dashing gallant of whom ladies begged souvenirs—a lock of hair, a button, an autograph.

At the Chickahominy, the men gazed in despair. The river was swollen. The ford Jeb had counted on was flooded high.

Jeb gave no sign that he was stunned by this setback. He ordered the column downriver to Forge Bridge, which, though in ruins, still had supports standing. Using boards from an old barn, a squad of scouts knocked together a crude walkway. It wobbled, swayed, but held together.

When the last man had crossed, the bridge was burned. The Federals reached the shore to see a solid span of flame. They gave up the chase.

Jeb rode ahead to report to General Lee. He rightly boasted of success.

He had defeated the enemy wherever he had met them. He had burned two hundred wagons, destroyed three big transports, captured 165 prisoners and 260 mules and horses—all at the cost of one man. The Federal losses ran into several million dollars.

A source of abiding triumph was his humiliation of the opposing cavalry, led by his father-in-law, General Philip St. George Cooke.

The sweep around McClellan and other raids equally spectacular later on won Jeb world-wide fame. Throughout his part in the war, the "gay cavalier" screened Lee's movements and scouted out the enemy's.

"Never did he bring me a piece of false information," declared Lee. To Lee, Jeb was "the eyes of the army."

As the months wore on, Jeb's ranks thinned. In May, 1864, tough Philip Sheridan advanced on Richmond with twelve thousand troops and the avowed purpose of crushing the Gray horsemen. Major General Stuart scraped up 4,500 men and flung them against the tremendous column, a column thirteen miles long.

At a shabby hamlet called Yellow Tavern, Jeb wedged his men between Richmond and the bluecoats. In the fighting, Jeb was shot and he died the following day in Richmond. Gone forever was the voice that rollicked through "Jine the Cavalry."

Gone forever was the "gay cavalier," riding at a gallop toward the enemy.

JAMES EWELL BROWN STUART

BORN: Patrick County, Virginia, February 6, 1833.
DIED: Richmond, Virginia, May 12, 1864.

THE ILLUSTRATION, PAGE 57: *Map of Stuart's route, June 13, 1862.*

Raphael Semmes
Rear Admiral, Confederate States of America

13

PIRATE IN GRAY

IN HER every line the 290th ship to slide from the Lairds shipyard in Birkenhead, England, was a superb war vessel. Of course, her well-paid builder did not boast of his masterpiece. English neutrality prohibited the building of men-of-war for foreign powers.

On the morning of July 29, 1862, the "290" departed Liverpool with a group of ladies and gentlemen. After lunch, the astonished guests were taken off by a tug. The ship was trimmed; the next night she vanished into the high seas.

Nine days later the "290" appeared off Terceira, an island in the Azores, and the masquerade ended. To her side came two consorts. One brought armament and stores. The other brought her American officers and captain. With a crew recruited on the spot, she set sail as the Confederate cruiser *Alabama*.

The South, lacking important shipyards, had to purchase ocean-going ships abroad. In the *Alabama*, the Confederacy had purchased (for $250,000) a craft as eager for action as a bent bow.

She had been created for one purpose: to prey upon Union commerce. Weighing about 1,000 tons, she was 230 feet in length, 32 feet in breadth, and 20 feet in depth. Her arms consisted of eight assorted guns.

She was built more for speed than combat. With a favorable wind and driven by two powerful engines, she could attain fifteen knots. A device raised her propeller so it did not drag when she was under sail only.

Her range was virtually unlimited. She was able to make all ordinary repairs on the seas, and hence avoid the delays and dangers of ports.

If the *Alabama* was the perfect weapon, her skipper, Raphael Semmes, was the perfect hand to wield her.

Semmes was master of many trades. Prior to the war, he had served as an officer of the U. S. Navy. At the same time he had found time to learn and practice law, and to write two books about the sea. He had skippered the first Confederate cruiser, *Sumter*, which before she wore out had taken fifteen prizes in six months.

Together Semmes and the *Alabama* swept the seas of Union merchantmen. No other ship and captain, before or since, dealt such fatal strokes to the shipping of a great nation.

AFTER a brief shakedown cruise, Semmes got about his favorite habit of attacking enemy commerce. He sailed for the mid-Atlantic and the New England whalers. Eleven days after assuming command, he captured his first prize. By the time winter gales threatened, he had destroyed ten ships.

He turned his prow toward the American coast. From Newfoundland he roved south to the Caribbean Sea and then to the Gulf of Mexico. Along the way he added seven more victims.

Against an unarmed foe, Semmes's practice was to remove crew and passengers and then set the ship ablaze. Later he released his prisoners at a convenient point of land.

Normally, he shied from trading shots with heavily armed ships. But on January 11, 1863, he sighted five warships off Galveston, Texas. To run might cost him the faith of his men. To engage all five was suicide.

Semmes hovered at a distance till one man-of-war, the *Hatteras*, steamed out to investigate. Shrewdly, Semmes lured her farther and farther from the squadron. At twilight, the enemy drew even.

Semmes greeted her with a broadside. He stood on the quarterdeck, ducking shots and encouraging his men.

"Give it to the rascals. Fire low, men. Don't be all night sinking that fellow!"

The two ships were of a size, though the *Alabama* had a slight edge in firepower. Thirteen minutes after the battle started, the *Hatteras* sank. Semmes rescued all her crew.

The outraged North sent forth cruisers to sink the "pirate." Semmes eluded all traps. By scanning the papers and letters of captured ships, he kept up with the movements of his pursuers and outwitted them.

He roamed the coast like a seawolf. Frightened merchants tried to disguise their cargoes with certificates of foreign ownership. They hoped thereby to gain the safety of a neutral. Semmes's legal training stood him in good stead. He knew his rights, and he readily saw through the many tricks to fool him. Genuine foreign cargoes and foreign ships he did not molest. By upholding international law, he reflected great credit upon himself and his country.

With forty-four ships added to his score, Semmes quit the American coast. Halfway around the world he hunted Union merchantmen, sinking ships as far east as the Indian Ocean and the China Sea.

Inevitably, the *Alabama* felt the strain of continuous duty. Her boiler burned out, her machinery wore loose. Semmes shaped course for Cherbourg, France, to repair her. On June 11, 1864, he entered the neutral port and met the Union man-of-war *Kearsarge*, one of the vessels ordered to track him down. Although the *Kearsarge* was in perfect condition, Semmes gave fight on Sunday morning, June 19.

People crowded to the heights above the city to witness the conflict. To catch a closer view, private yachts trailed the *Alabama* out beyond the neutral zone.

In almost all respects the two opponents were evenly matched. But the *Kearsarge*, unknown to Semmes, had chain armor on her sides.

While a mile apart, the *Alabama* opened fire with her hundred-pound pivot gun, and the *Kearsarge* promptly responded. The two ships closed, dueling in a circle that narrowed to five hundred yards in diameter. Semmes was surprised to see his shells explode harmlessly against the hull of the *Kearsarge*. He switched to solid shot. By then, alas, his ship was crippled.

On the eighth tour of the circle, the *Alabama* began to list. After an hour and a half of the fight to the death, she plunged beneath the ocean.

Semmes was picked out of the water

by an English yacht, and eventually he returned to the South. There he was promoted to rear admiral.

Enraged by his success, the North brought him to trial after the war. The charges were shamefully absurd, and he was set free by Presidential order.

Rotting beneath the waves today lie the ships Raphael Semmes sank in strict accordance with international law. He was patriot, scholar, destroyer. Beside him, the bold buccaneers of the Spanish Main appear like noisy amateurs.

In twenty-two months, as captain of the *Alabama*, he had taken two thousand prisoners, boarded 386 ships, and destroyed at least five million dollars worth of enemy property.

RAPHAEL SEMMES

> BORN: Charles County, Maryland, September 27, 1809.
> DIED: Point Clear, Alabama, August 30, 1877.

THE ILLUSTRATION, PAGE 61: *The "Alabama" (right) being sunk by the "Kearsarge" in the duel off Cherbourg.*

George Brinton McClellan
Major General, United States of America

14

BUILDER OF THE ARMY

THE COLONEL trembled with excitement as he handed the order to General George B. McClellan.

The chunky, red-haired Union commander read the single sheet with eyes widening. He stepped out of his tent to reread it in the sunlight. In a low, tight voice he questioned the colonel.

Was this some kind of joke?

No, the colonel answered. The order was genuine.

What McClellan held in his hand was Special Orders No. 191—*a Confederate order*. It was Robert E. Lee's in-

structions to his commanders for the opening stages of his first invasion of the North!

Two Union soldiers had discovered the fateful sheet in a meadow an hour earlier, wrapped around three cigars. How it had been lost, and by whom, would forever be among history's most tantalizing secrets.

The order was dated September 9, 1862. By now, four days later, the Confederate Army was divided into five columns.

McClellan seemed to grow a foot

taller. Fortune, which had always favored him above other men, had suddenly made him all knowing. The sheet of paper stripped Lee of his cunning and laid bare his plans.

McClellan threw up his arms triumphantly. "Now I know what to do!" he cried.

Moving swiftly, he could fall upon the Gray columns with awful accuracy and crush them one by one. The war would be over in a month!

But McClellan, a former railroad engineer and vice president, was noted for erecting defenses, not for rapid offensive strikes. At midnight he was still camped near Frederick City, Maryland, where the order was found. Painstakingly, he was getting everything ready.

He wired President Lincoln of the Confederates' doom. One line of the cable caught Lincoln's eye: *I . . . will catch them in their own trap if my men are equal to the emergency.*

Lincoln shook his head. General McClellan was already preparing an alibi for failure in battle. His men, not he, would be to blame.

When satisfied that everything was ready, McClellan gave chase. He knew exactly where to look. His Army of the Potomac would grind Lee's scattered Army of Northern Virginia into dust.

Proudly McClellan watched the Blue legions sweep forward. As brigade after brigade marched by him, the soldiers burst into cheers for "Little Mac." No officer was ever more popular with his troops.

In motion, the Army of the Potomac was a breath-taking sight. Tens of thousands of men shimmered across the landscape, jamming the roads, coloring the ground a Federal blue. Cavalry protected the flanks and scouted in the front. Layered inward were the infantry, artillery, and supply wagons. Strung in the rear came stragglers slowed by fear or weariness, untested recruits, and washerwomen. Hurrying to catch up were men who had been plundering farms when their regiments broke camp.

It was *his* army. He, George McClellan, had put it together. After First Bull Run (Manassas), he had taken over the defense of Washington, supreme Northern commander at thirty-four! From a beaten, panicked mob he had built an army of 168,000—the biggest, grandest army in the world! His name in the land rang louder than Abraham Lincoln's.

Yet, somehow, George McClellan had not been able to make his army fight as well as it drilled. Earlier in the year, his plodding Peninsula campaign had failed to capture Richmond, and he had been relieved of command. His brilliant engineer's mind kept wanting the perfect battle machine. If only he had more time to prepare it . . .

◦⃝

Now he was being given a second chance to turn the wheels of war. To guide him, George McClellan had Special Orders No. 191. It was the blueprint to the mind of Robert E. Lee, the road map to victory.

By the time McClellan got his army going, Lee had learned of the lost order. He retreated behind South Mountain and anxiously awaited the return of his separated columns.

McClellan found him near the town of Sharpsburg, on the night of September 15. Tracked and at bay, Lee had braced for a stand. He placed his back to the Potomac River and spread his thin ranks along a winding creek, the Antietam.

Instead of attacking, McClellan spent all the next day positioning his great army. "I will not move until I know everything is ready," he declared.

That one day of getting everything ready cost the North a chance to end the war at Antietam. By nightfall, most of Lee's far-flung columns had returned to him.

Just before dawn of September 17, McClellan finally attacked. Along a four-mile front, his seventy thousand splendidly equipped troops faced forty thousand tired and ragged Southerners. As usual, however, he believed the Southerners outnumbered him. Hence he kept one-third of his force in reserve and never used it.

The battle of Antietam was a standoff. It lives as the bloodiest engagement ever fought on American soil up till that time. The North suffered twelve thousand dead and wounded. Lee lost more than a fifth of his army.

Although Lee's invasion had been thrown back, Abraham Lincoln was bitterly disappointed. His commander had failed to pursue the Confederates. Weeks later, as McClellan was carefully getting ready to fight anew, Lincoln removed him.

Never again was he entrusted with a field command. In 1864 he resigned his commission to run for President on the Democratic ticket. Lincoln defeated him handily. In 1878 he reentered politics and was elected Governor of New Jersey.

McClellan's great achievements as an organizer have been overshadowed by his caution as a fighter. After the disaster of First Bull Run, he restored the nation's confidence. He molded the Union forces into the Army of the Potomac. He fortified Washington.

Today he is remembered for his failures. He was the young engineer of whom Lincoln said: "He seems to have a special talent for the stationary engine."

In the first year of war he was the North's number one soldier. Before the end of the second year, he was in eclipse.

Why? Perhaps because he rose too rapidly to the top command. He had no time to master war gradually, as had those who followed him. He had to go by the book. The book can teach you how to maneuver, but not how to fight.

Whatever his shortcomings, McClellan forged the Army of the Potomac and breathed into it spirit. Nothing broke that spirit, not even a succession of unsuccessful commanders led off by McClellan himself.

❧⋅❧⋅❧ • ❧⋅❧⋅❧

GEORGE BRINTON McCLELLAN

> Born: Philadelphia, Pennsylvania, December 3, 1826.
> Died: Orange, New Jersey, October 29, 1885.

The Illustration, Page 65: *Northern rifles and a military drum: Sharp's carbine, at left; Green's breech-loader, at right.*

Ambrose Powell Hill
Lieutenant General, Confederate States of America

15

UP CAME HILL

THE ARMY of Northern Virginia rolled to its first invasion of the North missing one wheel. General Ambrose Hill was under arrest. He went into Maryland on foot, tagging behind his "Light Division" with the stragglers and washerwomen.

Dust coated his flannel shirt and powdered his red beard. It was not the dust, however, that irritated the thin-skinned major general. He was sure he had been wronged. And he was determined to have his rights, no matter how long it took.

The trouble had started that morning. Stonewall Jackson had disliked the pace at which Hill's division marched. The front trod too briskly, in Stonewall's opinion. That meant the rear would ravel. He had ordered the lead brigade to halt so the files might close.

Hill, always ready for a fight, had come up in a temper.

"If you're going to give the orders to my division, you don't need me!" he had stormed, unbuckling his sword.

Jackson had declined the proffered blade. "Consider yourself under arrest for neglect of duty," he had answered.

So the Light Division had crossed the Potomac under a new commander. Powell Hill, "mad as a bull," strode in the rear, unbowed and unconsulted.

When the army rested outside Frederick City, he asked for a copy of the charges against him. Jackson replied by letter that charges would be furnished "should the interests of the service require your case to be brought before the Court Martial." In the meantime, Hill was instructed to remain with his division.

Hill seethed at the injustice—disgrace without appeal. For a while he considered entering Lee's tent at Best's Grove and demanding a trial.

Patriotism overruled pride. He would keep himself available. In the campaign about to unfold, Jackson might need his sure hand.

The army, divided into five parts, quit Frederick under Lee's fateful document Special Orders 191. There was no missing the scent of battle now. Hill champed like a warhorse. Rather than lose out on a minute of action, he got one of Jackson's aides, Kyd Douglas, to plead for him.

"No one can command Hill's division as well as he," Douglas pointed out. Without comment, Jackson rein-

stated his hot-tempered subordinate.

Five days later the Union arsenal at Harper's Ferry surrendered to Jackson. He promptly marched north to rejoin the main body of the army. Hill and his Light Division stayed behind to handle the spoils—eleven thousand prisoners and twelve thousand stands of arms.

At six-thirty in the morning of September 17, Hill received an urgent summons from Lee—*Come up!* A Union private had found a copy of Special Orders 191. Acting upon this information, McClellan had moved with unaccustomed speed. Now Lee's thirty thousand faced "Little Mac's" seventy thousand along the Antietam. The Light Division was needed desperately in that woefully thin Gray line.

Hill posted one brigade at Harper's Ferry to finish up there. The other five he had on the road within the hour.

A. P. Hill was "coming up," and with him the Light Division, strongest of Lee's divisions!

The men of Hill stepped with special verve—the "forward spirit" with which their leader had inspired them. Cast aside were Jackson's rigid rules of march prescribing regular rest periods. Stragglers who collapsed from the pace were left by the road. "Come up when you can—"

The general whom Stonewall considered a bad marcher was treading to the silent beat of glory. A. P. Hill was marching to rescue an army and save a nation. Relentlessly he drove his men toward the rumble of guns. "Close up! Close up!"

The temper which had been his weakness became his staff. His orders crackled. The men caught his fire.

⁓

ALONG the Antietam a phenomenon was occurring. Powerful Union divisions had won nearly all the high ground south and east of the town of Sharpsburg. The Confederate right was quivering and ready to go. The entire Gray line was slender and taut as a heart string. Yet nowhere did it break.

For a battery of the Light Division had arrived. The Southerners braced to the cry. "A. P. Hill is close behind and coming up!"

Once Jefferson Davis had referred to the slightly built Hill as "little A. P. Hill," though he stood five feet ten inches. At four o'clock on that September afternoon Hill looked as big as all salvation coming down the road to Sharpsburg in his bright red battle shirt.

His column could not have taken any prizes. It was bedraggled and opened wide. It had covered sixteen miles, sloughing off two thousand men during the grueling trek.

Lee threw his arms around Hill in a rare display of emotion. Then he soberly gave his orders.

Hill hurled his hard-core three thousand into the fray. Through fields of tall corn he sent a brigade wearing blue uniforms captured at Harper's Ferry.

The Union regiments hesitated at what appeared to be their own troops. Bullets and then panic hit them in close order. The Union left caved in. The Union regiments were driven out of Sharpsburg and down to the banks of the Antietam. The ghastly bloodletting ended at nightfall.

Although the Confederate invasion was stopped, the Army of Northern Virginia escaped destruction. Lee had kept it alive, but it was Hill and his Light Division that snatched it from the jaws of death.

The following spring, upon Jackson's passing, the army's two corps were increased to three. Hill was given the third corps, and promoted to lieutenant general. As a corps commander, he fared irregularly, serving until tragically near the peace. He was killed rallying his men at Petersburg the week before the surrender.

He never had the chance to contest the charges which resulted in his period of arrest. Neither did he ever completely mend the rift with Stonewall Jackson.

Yet his was the last name uttered by Jackson—and by Lee.

"Order A. P. Hill to prepare for action!" cried the sinking Jackson.

On his deathbed Lee called, "Tell Hill he must come up!"

In 1892 a statue of Hill was unveiled in Richmond. He was the fourth war leader thus honored by the South. But it remained for his spirit to be captured by the words of an aging veteran.

"A. P. Hill was either there or always came up."

AMBROSE POWELL HILL

> BORN: Culpeper, Virginia, November 9, 1825.
> DIED: Petersburg, Virginia, April 2, 1865.

THE ILLUSTRATION, PAGE 69: *A Union charge against heavy Confederate fire.*

Ambrose Everett Burnside
Major General, United States of America

16

MASSACRE AT FREDERICKSBURG

GENERAL AMBROSE BURNSIDE gazed moodily down from the heights overlooking Antietam Creek. A triple-arched stone bridge spanned the water below him. Before the day was done, the little crossing would become a famous landmark. As "Burnside's Bridge" it would forever symbolize the indecision of one man.

A courier galloped up with an order from Burnside's superior, General George McClellan. Burnside let an aide accept the paper. He knew what it contained. Three like it had already reached him. "Assault the bridge!"

Since dawn fighting had raged everywhere but in this sector, the Union left. Here an ominous quiet ruled.

On the steeply banked shore opposite him, Burnside detected nothing of the enemy. He knew they were there, though. They had chased his scouts from the approaches to the bridge all morning. Firing from less than a hunded yards away, Gray sharpshooters killed anything in their sights.

Burnside understood about small arms. Before the war he had invented a breach-loading rifle. To throw a charge across that bridge would be murder.

73

So he despaired and delayed, trying to bring himself to do what McClellan wanted.

Another courier rode up. It was McClellan's inspector-general. "Take the bridge—at bayonet point if necessary!"

Burnside whirled in anguish. "McClellan seems to think I am not trying my best to carry this bridge!" he shouted. "You are the third or fourth one who has been to me this morning with similar orders."

But this time he issued the command. It was 1:00 P.M., September 17, 1862, when the first wave raced across. Four precious hours had been wasted since McClellan's first order to cross was received.

Five hundred men fell in the charge through the narrow bottleneck of stone. The survivors fought onto the opposite bank and seemed on the verge of smashing the enemy. Suddenly Confederate reinforcements, just up from Harper's Ferry, rushed onto the field and stopped the Northerners cold. The battle of Antietam ended in a deadlock.

Later the truth came out. Had Burnside assaulted when first ordered, his corps would have faced a mere six hundred Confederates! His four hours of delay had thrown away a golden opportunity to end the war.

Less than three months after Antietam, the powers in Washington removed McClellan. Burnside, a popular general without political ambitions, found himself the new commander of the Army of the Potomac.

It was a responsibility he had twice refused, out of loyalty to McClellan. The two men were old friends. For his prewar job with the Illinois Central Railroad, Burnside could thank McClellan, who was a vice president. With his good friend fallen from grace, Burnside felt it unpatriotic to refuse again.

No soldier ever prepared to defend his country in a more disturbed state of mind. Haunting him was the bloody bridge at the Antietam. Deep inside, he knew his hours of dawdling had let victory trickle off.

There his mistake had been in trying to protect his men. That mistake was soon to beget a bigger one—one resulting in the slaughter of six thousand brave Northern soldiers. For Ambrose Burnside determined to hesitate no more. If ever again victory could be bought at the expense of a few hundred lives, he would spend them.

He rearranged the Army of the Potomac into three grand divisions and went after Lee. His plan was to cross the Rappahannock River at the town of

Fredericksburg, meet his supplies there, and march rapidly on Richmond—a sound maneuver.

Success hinged on swiftness, and swiftness hinged on getting across the Rappahannock. When the army reached the river, there were no pontoon boats for a bridge. Not until two long weeks later did the boats arrive.

But then Lee was ready.

His lines stretched for five miles along the hills which lay about Fredericksburg. The strongest entrenchment was at the lowest hill, Marye's Heights, behind the town. An unbreakable arc of Confederate steel gripped the area—north, south, and west. From the east came Ambrose Burnside and the Army of the Potomac.

For two days the Northerners moved across the river and into the level plain of the valley. On the morning of December 13 a fog blanketed their final preparations. The Confederates, secure in their hills, saw nothing.

Abruptly at ten o'clock the fog parted. Eighty thousand Confederates looked down at the "grandest military scene of the war."

Masses of bayonets glistened in the warm sunlight. Gun carriages rattled, horses champed. Flags and guidons unfurled. Officers in new uniforms shuttled their men in last-minute positioning. One hundred and sixteen thousand Northerners poised for the attack.

Burnside studied the open slopes, almost bare of concealment or cover. He did not hesitate. As if to wipe out the memory of Antietam, he ordered the bugles to sound.

He fed his men to the Confederates. Not in one assault, or in two. *Six* times the Blue lines heroically sprang for the enemy. Six times they were overwhelmed, like climbers in an avalanche.

Night ended the madness. In a sunken road at Marye's Hill, six thousand Union corpses were heaped. Altogether, the Union had lost twelve thousand men.

Burnside wanted to lead in person one last charge the following morning. His generals argued him out of it. Having lost the confidence of both his officers and men, he saw no alternative. He asked to be relieved, blaming none but himself for the massacre.

Smaller commands, which were more to his liking, were given him. Shortly before Lee's surrender, he returned to private life. There his reputation for honesty and his great personal charm made him wealthy and famous.

He became president of several railroads and entered public life. The people of Rhode Island elected him governor and later United States Senator.

Curiously, it is neither his failures nor his successes which endure in our talk today. It is the special flare of his whiskers.

With Ambrose Burnside's beard—full at the sides and bare at the chin—originated the word *sideburns*.

AMBROSE EVERETT BURNSIDE

> BORN: Liberty, Indiana, May 23, 1824.
> DIED: Bristol, Rhode Island, September 13, 1881.

THE ILLUSTRATION, PAGE 73: *The bridge at Antietam.*

76

Clara Barton
Relief Carrier

17

HEY, MISS BARTON!

IN THE FIRST week of the war a trainload of roughly used Massachusetts militiamen arrived in Washington. At the station to greet them was a small woman who radiated welcome.

"It's Miss Barton!" exclaimed a young private, his head swathed in bandages. "Hey," he cried, leaning out the window. "Hey, Miss Barton!"

Clara Barton waved cheerfully. Ten years before, the boy had been one of her pupils.

There were others who remembered her, and whom she remembered. Young men from Worcester, her home town; and from North Oxford, one of the communities where she had taught school.

The youths were overjoyed to see her broad, friendly face and merry, dark brown eyes. She seemed to bring to a cold strange city all the warmth of home.

This was as Clara Barton intended. She had heard that the regiment had been attacked by Secessionists in Baltimore. At the depot she learned the details. Before being routed, the mob had killed three soldiers, wounded thirty, and dumped all the unit's baggage.

"We ain't got nothing except what's on our backs," lamented one boy. He pinched his flannel blouse. "And is it hot!"

Clara Barton started to sympathize. All at once her words sounded wrong. Cheer and understanding were fine, but not enough. Determined to *do* something, Clara went to the market and bought a great amount of food. In her sunny rooms on T Street she ripped up sheets, towels, and handkerchiefs and packed them in a large basket.

That evening she passed at the Washington Infirmary with forty ragged, bloody volunteers who said "everything but their prayers."

In the morning, Sunday, churchgoers parted for an odd parade. Out in front marched Clara, nose high in boxes. Behind her stepped five porters bearing huge baskets loaded with food. Clara distributed the delicacies to her Massachusetts boys, who were not yet "well used to hardtack."

With the impulse to relieve distress, Clara Barton, an unknown copyist in the Patent Office, had begun her career of service. It was to continue fifty years after the Civil War and make her one of the century's most honored women.

More and more soldiers steamed into Washington. Clara cheered them, wrote letters for them, and supplied them with comforts.

When her money ran low, she sent an appeal to her home-town newspaper, the Worcester *Daily Spy*. The reaction was like a cloudburst. Patriotic groups, churches, sewing circles, and private citizens showered her with supplies. Word of her needs spread through New England. Her rooms bulged with clothing, bandages, jellies, preserved fruits, canned soup, coffee, brandy, lint, tobacco, and drugs.

Clara had to hire space in a warehouse. Good intentions had grown into a distributing agency.

❦

DURING August and September she had her hands full. Errands of mercy took her on an unending round of Washington hospitals, railroad platforms, and wharves. She recruited friends and relatives to aid her receive, sort, and store the influx of barrels, bundles, and boxes.

When the soldiers moved from camp to battlefield, Clara pleaded to go with them. The surgeon general stubbornly refused her permission. Clara was just as stubborn. She pounded on doors and snipped at red tape. In and out of government departments she trudged until she obtained all the necessary passes.

When our armies fought on Cedar Mountain, I broke the shackles and went to the field, she wrote in her diary. *And so began my work.*

The Army field hospital at Cedar Mountain was running short of dressings when Brigade Surgeon James L. Dunn beheld a wagon train approaching. Mounted on the lead wagon was a small woman of forty, attired in a jacket, dark print skirt, and kerchief. Among her boxes and bundles were large quantities of dressings.

"I thought that night if heaven ever sent a holy angel, she must be one, her assistance was so timely," recalled Dr. Dunn.

Few women got as close to the firing. Time after time Clara reached the field while the battle raged. At Antietam a bullet nipped her sleeve and killed the soldier she was attending. Before Fredricksburg part of her skirts were shot away by a piece of an exploding shell.

Ignoring danger, she brought her perfectly packed supplies of food, clothing, and medicine to the front before anyone knew she was on her way.

With her knack of appearing as if from heaven, Union soldiers began calling her the "Angel of the Battlefield." Another and less accurate nickname was the "American Florence Nightingale."

Although she tended the wounded and was briefly superintendent of nurses with General Ben Butler, Clara was not primarily a nurse. She cooperated with various relief associations like the Sanitary and Christian Commissions, and the nurses corps of Dorothea Dix. But she never belonged to any group.

Neither did she become officially part of the Union Army. She disliked being under anyone else's authority. Her independence enabled her to meet emergencies successfully.

She brought relief *where* it was needed, *when* it was needed. Government supplies were normally far to the rear when her wagons halted by the wounded.

This was Clara Barton's great contribution. She answered a need until the regular medical aid and supplies came up.

"I could run risks," she maintained. "It made no difference if I were shot or taken prisoner. I tried to fill the gap."

Her acts of mercy did not stop with Appomattox. The war had left too many loose ends dangling in tears. For four years Clara directed a search for missing soldiers.

Families learned where loved ones were buried. In many cases men falsely branded as deserters were cleared of that disgrace. She published lists of men who died in Andersonville and other prisoner-of-war camps. Through her industry, twenty thousand missing soldiers were identified.

For all this, Clara's reputation was still in the building. Her greatest accomplishment lay in the future—in establishing a permanent agency for giving relief in emergencies, to people of the North and South, in peace and in war.

In 1881 Clara Barton founded the American Red Cross, and for nearly twenty-five years she served as its president.

CLARA BARTON

Born: Oxford, Massachusetts, December 25, 1821.
Died: Glen Echo, Maryland, April 12, 1912.

The Illustration, Page 77: *Earliest first aid kit introduced in America by Clara Barton.*

David Dixon Porter
Rear Admiral, United States of America

18

SECRET WEAPON

ONCE UPON A TIME there were an acting rear admiral and a harmless old coal barge. The acting rear admiral yearned to be a *real* rear admiral, and the coal barge wanted to be an ironclad.

How they achieved their ambitions is the nearest thing to a fairy tale to come out of the Civil War.

The acting rear admiral's name was David Porter. He had his first command, the Mississippi Squadron. His ships controlled the great river, except at Port Hudson, Louisiana, and at Vicksburg, Mississippi.

Alas, in the past two weeks Porter had lost two first-class ships. His ram, *Queen of the West*, had been treacherously run aground and captured. To add insult to injury, the Confederates used the *Queen* to help sink his new, 170-foot ironclad, *Indianola*.

The sunken ship could undo him, could wipe away a lifetime of naval service, if the Confederates ever used the ship against him. He would be dropped back to commander, his former rank. He dreaded being lost in the scramble of junior officers.

Sitting in the cabin of his flagship, the *Blackhawk*, Porter mulled over the embarrassing situation. The facts were hardly comforting. The previous night the *Indianola* had been sunk below Warrenton, Mississippi. But how badly was she damaged?

Certainly the Confederates would try to pump and raise her. With both the *Queen* and the *Indianola* in their possession, the Confederates had practically a new fleet. One that might drive Porter's from the Mississippi!

Even stuck fast in the mud, the *Indianola* was dangerous. Her guns could be salvaged for other ships.

What could be done? Porter and his fleet were on the Yazoo River with the army. And on the Yazoo he must stay, though his chances of being confirmed rear admiral hovered by the sunken *Indianola*.

A log floated across the round patch of water revealed by the cabin porthole. Porter watched it ride past on the current. All at once he went bounding on deck, shouting orders. The driftwood had touched off a fantastic scheme.

There was much work and scant time. The entire squadron laid to. Trees were chopped down, trimmed, and hauled to the anchorage. Pork barrels were collected from the army, and two hogsheads were commandeered from a neighborhood barn.

A gigantic craft began to take shape. The logs were lashed to a coal barge to form sides. Two tremendous wheelhouses were fashioned of the barrels. Log guns slanted ominously from log casements. A pair of leaky old boats were hung from davits. The two hogsheads, positioned like smokestacks, rounded out the illusion.

As the weird dummy neared completion, late news of the *Indianola* arrived. The ironclad lay with her forecastle under a foot of shoal water near the plantation of Joseph Davis, brother of the President. The Confederates were busy removing her guns. More critical was the information about the *Queen*. She had gone downstream after pumps.

Porter hurried the last refinements on his floating stage. Across the wheelhouse someone painted an anti-Confederate slogan. An American flag was hoisted at the stern, and a pennant with a skull and crossbones snapped at the bow.

From a distance the coal barge looked like the ironclad *Lafayette*, which had just reached the fleet from St. Louis. Porter pranced in delight.

At midnight the harmless hulk, three hundred feet long, was towed close to the water batteries of Vicksburg. A single sailor climbed aboard and lighted the big iron kettles inside each "smokestack." Tar and oakum caught instantly, puffing black smoke into the night. The sailor jumped off and set the dummy adrift.

Down at Vicksburg the sentries were alerted to the approach of a new supership. As soon as the huge silhouette came within gunshot, the batteries unleashed earth-trembling salvos. Shell after shell hit home. Yet they had no effect. The dark shape was as unsinkable as a gigantic cork.

The bombardment did not let up till the "monster ironclad" was beyond range. All the while she made her way in ghostly silence, disdaining to fire in reply.

A report of the monster flew through Vicksburg. The citizens sobered in their joy over the capture of the *Indianola* and the *Queen*. Something colossal and spooky was on the water.

Couriers galloped ahead to Joseph Davis' plantation. The crew of the Confederate ram *William H. Webb* had gone aboard the *Indianola* in an effort to remove her guns. When they heard about the supership, they decided to blow up their prize and clear out.

⁓

MEANTIME, the mock ironclad, still some miles above the *Indianola*, caught an eddy and ran against the bank. Some Yank soldiers had been riding on the shores to see the fun. They heaved and strained and got the pile of barrels and logs back into the current by daybreak.

Silently the ghost ship continued on her course toward the *Indianola*.

At Warrenton, two crewmen of the Confederate *Queen* were at anchor when they beheld a great ironclad break through the mists of dawn and bear down upon them.

The men wailed. The captain bellowed. The fasts were cut, and the *Queen* swung down the river. But her steam was low. For a while the dummy drifted at an equal speed.

The *Queen* finally outdistanced her huge pursuer and reached the *Indianola*. The enemy was close behind! The men on the *Indianola* scurried back to the *Webb* without having blown up a sand fly. Together the two Confederate ships fled south.

So it happened that on February 26, 1863, a coal barge ruled a hundred miles of the mighty Mississippi. By bluff and good luck, an acting admiral had escaped disgrace. He had chased the Confederates from his sunken ironclad.

When they learned of the trick, the people of Vicksburg were enraged. Southern newspapers sneered for days at the naval authorities. Couldn't they tell a barge with fancy airs from a genuine ironclad?

Eventually, the *Queen* was recaptured from the Confederates. And the *Indianola* was raised by the North after Vicksburg surrendered on July 4, 1863.

On that date Rear Admiral David Porter officially got rid of the word "acting."

And the "monster ironclad" turned back into a coal barge.

DAVID DIXON PORTER

Born: Chester, Pennsylvania, June 8, 1813.
Died: Washington, February 13, 1891.

The Illustration, Page 81: *Admiral Porter's dummy ironclad.*

John Singleton Mosby
Colonel, Confederate States of America

19

GRAY GHOST

NIGHT . . . quick footsteps in the rain . . . the stealthy creak of a door opening. . . . a pair of piercing blue eyes.

Lieutenant John Mosby yanked the quilt from the slumbering form of Brigadier General Edwin H. Stoughton. Grinning wickedly, he removed one of his own white gloves, tossed back the Union officer's nightshirt, and delivered a resounding slap.

Stoughton twisted up in bed, swearing in fury and pain.

"General," asked Mosby sharply. "Did you ever hear of Mosby?"

"Yes, have you caught the devil?"

Mosby's voice was a cat's purr. "No, he has caught you."

Stoughton rubbed sleep-reddened eyes. He swore, groaned, and sagged back on the bed.

He envisioned his entire force, the 2nd Vermont Brigade, in Confederate hands. If Mosby was here in Fairfax Courthouse, Virginia, then so was his chief, Jeb Stuart. And the dreaded Stonewall Jackson could not be far behind.

"Is Fitzhugh Lee with you?" asked Stoughton, his face brightening. "He will make sure I am well treated. We were classmates at West Point."

"I will take you to him," lied Mosby.

For an hour Mosby and his rangers stayed in the Union-held village without having to fire a shot. They operated in silent, beautiful harmony. Then Mosby's white glove sliced forward. The rangers and all the prisoners and horses they could handle trotted from Fairfax Courthouse.

Out beyond the last home Stoughton grasped what had taken place. "This is a bold thing you have done," he marveled. "But our cavalry will soon be after you."

Mosby's reply was an icy smile. He had taken twenty-nine rangers twenty-five miles behind enemy lines, melted through strong pickets, and kidnaped a Union general and one hundred others from the midst of five thousand of their comrades!

To hoodwink his pursuers, he started north. After a few hundred yards, he swung left around the infantry camps, and got on the pike toward Centerville.

About fifty prisoners slipped away in the night rain before the column reached Confederate lines. Nonetheless, Mosby brought in Stoughton, two captains, and thirty privates, along with fifty-eight horses selected from officers' stables.

Lincoln took the humiliation philosophically. "I can always make more brigadier generals," he said wryly. "But I can't make horses."

General Jeb Stuart was delighted by his bold scout. "It is a feat unparalleled in the war," he exulted.

The Fairfax Courthouse raid on March 9, 1863, was Mosby's most brilliant exploit, though neither his first nor his last. Throughout the conflict he sorely vexed the Union armies in Virginia. He plundered supply wagons, cut telegraph wires, derailed trains, stole money. His rangers struck like the hammer of Thor and then faded into the countryside like gray ghosts.

Twice, the Yanks captured him. Twice, he escaped. The enemy failed to recognize the slender, wiry little man. Apparently the North imagined the famous ranger must have the size to match his reputation.

Mosby never weighed more than 125 pounds, even with the chip on his shoulder. A dandy in his fighting togs, he wore a cape lined with scarlet, an ostrich plume that curled from a gray felt hat after the style of his idol, Jeb Stuart. His white gloves, which stood out like lanterns, flashed signals in silence and darkness.

On any given foray, his detachment seldom numbered more than eighty. Yet the rangers never lacked fire power. Mosby himself was a galloping arsenal.

Six-shooters were his meat. He carried two slung from holsters and two more handy on the saddle. He scorned sabers as a rattling nuisance. His men were similarly armed. Some even tucked a third pair of .44 Colts into their boots.

❧

AFTER the Fairfax Courthouse raid, he was promoted to captain, and two weeks later, to major. He also got what he valued above rank: an independent command.

It wasn't a standing command, like General John Morgan's. And it wasn't much on button polishing. Cutthroats, freebooters, and deserters gathered about him, as well as farmers, cavalrymen on leave, bankers, and pink-cheeked boys.

There were no drills or dull camp routine, for there were no camps. The rangers boarded pretty much where they pleased. But there was plenty of loot.

Mosby and his men took full advantage of the partisan ranger law. This allowed the splitting of captured public property among the captors. The rangers didn't hesitate to divide personal property, too.

Horse thieves, robbers, irregulars, guerrillas, the North called them. Partisan Rangers, they called themselves. Mosby considered his men an arm of the military, properly enrolled as Company A, 43rd Battalion, Partisan Rangers.

The little four-gun gamecock and his men galloped on raid after raid far within Union lines. If surrounded by the enemy, they simply faded away, each man shifting for himself. The smallness of the band simplified the getaway.

Whenever the Yankees gave chase, they found themselves hunting phantoms. Northern Virginia, south of the Potomac and east of the Blue Ridge Mountains, became known as "Mosby's Confederacy." Here a ranger could always find supplies, a fresh horse, or a hideout.

Mosby exasperated the Union generals, especially George Custer. The Northerner had six captured rangers killed while he sat in his saddle savoring a bunch of plums. Mosby hanged seven

Northern prisoners in reprisal, and there were no more executions.

When Lee surrendered, Mosby was a colonel commanding eight hardy companies numbering eight hundred rangers. He disbanded his men on April 21, 1865. Not until February of the following year was he himself pardoned.

He resumed his law practice, which had been interrupted by the war. In 1878, he received the appointment as consul at Hong Kong, where he stayed until 1885. In the years following he became a land agent in Colorado and assistant attorney for the Department of Justice.

He died in Washingon at the age of eighty-three, a respected lawyer and a formidable foe in the courts.

His worth as a Confederate soldier is tallied in the official papers of Robert E. Lee. The name most praised there is not Jackson or Hill or Stuart.

It is John Singleton Mosby.

JOHN SINGLETON MOSBY

BORN: Edgemont, Virginia, December 6, 1833.
DIED: Washington, May 30, 1916.

THE ILLUSTRATION, PAGE 85: *Southern lances, battleflags and officer's buckle.*

John Pelham

Major, Confederate States of America

20

THE SPLENDID BOY

THEY SAID OF Major John Pelham that he looked sixteen, that he blushed often, and that he boasted only once.

That once was when somebody had captured a gun of Jeb Stuart's horse artillery. Pelham, the proud organizer and leader of the scrappy little artillery force, boiled with resentment.

"We've never lost a gun! No, sir!" he boasted. And the very next day he nearly ate those words.

A slain horse had stalled one of his howitzers in an open field. Pelham worked furiously to disengage the dead animal. As he unfastened the last strap, a bullet grooved the air by his golden-brown head.

A squadron of Union cavalry had been pecking at his batteries all day. Sharpshooters would dash forward, fire, and retreat behind a wood. The lanky young Alabamian never had time to get off a shot.

"We've taken enough," he growled. "Sergeant Dabney, run everything but the other howitzer to the rear. We're going forward."

The Yanks discharged their carbines and retreated. Instantly Pelham spurred for the wood, trailed by the wildly bouncing howitzer. At the trees, the horses were unhitched and the piece pulled by hand through the thick undergrowth.

Pelham, his smooth cheeks flushed with battle heat, ordered a double load of canister.

A few hundred yards away the Yankees rested unaware. They never dreamed anyone would be so reckless as to drag a cannon into the wood. Eight of them died under the howitzer's blast of iron. Ten dropped wounded. The rest fled.

Pelham and his men raced from the wood with the enemy colors and several bewildered prisoners. The howitzer was pulled out, the horses hitched to it, and all galloped back to the battery.

It had been one of those daring feats which Pelham was continually performing, and which made him the darling of Stuart's cavalry. He aroused admiration without jealousy. His manly courage, modesty, and boyish good looks won over everybody.

"We loved him because he was a boy and we feared him because he was a man," one cannoneer put it.

"What Pelham did was always the very best that could be done," maintained Jeb Stuart.

Pelham returned his commander's regard. "There never was anybody like Stuart," he vowed.

The taciturn Stonewall Jackson rhapsodized when he beheld the youth at the Battle of Sharpsburg. Although a mere captain then, Pelham handled the artillery on the left wing of the army.

"With a Pelham on each flank, I believe I could whip the world!" exulted Stonewall.

Admirers dubbed him "the boy major," "the boy knight," "the South's boy hero." If he longed to be "the boy general," his disappointment did not break surface.

After the Seven Days, Stuart recommended his promotion, writing, *No field grade, in either cavalry or artillery, is too high for him.*

But the officials in Richmond saw the beardless Alabamian as "far too young for high command."

Stubbornly, Stuart pressed for his favorite. "No veteran in age has ever shown more coolness and better judgment in the sphere of duty," he argued.

To which Lee added: "No one deserves promotion more than Major Pelham."

PELHAM's ardor for fighting was not dulled by the slowness of official recognition. In combat, the blushing youth became a whirling demon. While his men sponged and loaded and rammed, he darted from gun to gun. "That's it, man! That's it!" he would shout.

He covered ground with uncanny speed. His face streaked with sweat and grime and dust, he damned and congratulated, unmindful of danger. His one concern was to maintain a steady outpouring of shot.

"Smack into 'em that time! Give it to 'em again, Burwell! Steady, Turner!"

Mature men drew inspiration from the blond, panting youth in the powder-blackened uniform. As he flew back and forth, his gaze swept the front unceasingly. On his lips was a peculiar battle smile.

No matter how fast General Stuart's cavalry traveled, the boy major stayed apace. His horses sped their ton-and-a-half loads through "impassable" fords and over rutted fields. The guns were always at the front when Stuart wanted them.

Besides this gift for arriving on time, Pelham had an almost mystical sense for choosing position. Stonewall Jackson granted him a privilege given to no other of Jackson's officers: the right to select his own spot on the battlefield.

He was a virtuoso of the cannon, a player in perfect tune with his instruments. The Stuart horse artillery composed a few pieces only—frequently but two howitzers and a Blakely. With this kind of light, maneuverable battery, Pelham performed at his best. He doted on a running battle in which he flashed from ridge to ridge. He would stop, hurl a round or two at the enemy, and then gallop on.

"He didn't look as though he could order anybody to be killed," remarked a girl who had fallen under his spell. "His face was all tenderness and softness. I used to say to myself: 'A man like that—this boy?' That is really what he was—a boy, a splendid boy."

The boy who killed so joyfully had a profound religious faith. He attended church and camp prayer meetings whenever possible. Belle Boyd, the spy, gave him a Bible which he carried all through his service. Its flyleaf bore the inscription in Belle's hand:

I know thou are loved by another now,
I know thou wilt never be mine—

Another was lovely Sally Dandridge. Pelham was never to be Sally's, either.

"I will not die in this war," he had confided to a friend. And, indeed, it seemed that a creature so blessed in all aspects must be in divine care.

But at Kelly's Ford, Virginia, a shell exploded in a cornfield, and suddenly Major Pelham's saddle was empty.

He was twenty-two years old when war began, twenty-four when he fell.

Jeb Stuart heard what had happened while directing a countercharge.

The boy—the splendid boy—was dead.

Stuart bowed his head and wept.

JOHN PELHAM

BORN: Cane Creek, Alabama, September 14, 1838.
DIED: Culpeper, Virginia, March 17, 1863.

THE ILLUSTRATION, PAGE 89: *A Confederate howitzer.*

George Armstrong Custer
Major General, United States of America

21

DANGER WAS HIS BLIND SPOT

THE CONFEDERATE cavalry bared sabers and swept across the field, screaming the shrill, terrifying Rebel yell. The Union line buckled. Order disappeared in swirling clashes of pistol and saber.

Frantically, the Union leaders rallied their men. The Yanks re-formed, countercharged. In the foremost point of Blue rode a young lieutenant with long yellow curls streaming from under a mangy straw hat.

The Gray horsemen yielded ground, grudgingly at first, then in full retreat. The Yanks reined up, winded, arm-weary, jubilant.

The boy in the straw hat rode on alone, his face shining with an odd light. Into the retiring enemy he galloped, unaware that his comrades had quit to rest. A cloud of dust swallowed him and the Confederates.

Suddenly he emerged, grinning. He lifted a bloody sword. George Armstrong Custer had felt the thrill of his first cavalry charge.

The skirmish that day at Aldie, Virginia, was little distinguished from a hundred others—except in two respects. It trumpeted to the world the presence of a slim, headstrong soldier who was as thirsty for war as a drawn saber. And it proved "Custer's luck" was as good as ever.

The broad-brimmed straw hat, exactly like those worn by the enemy, had allowed him to plunge rashly amid the Gray and emerge with his hide.

Luck had already won the handsome youth a brief promotion to General McClellan's staff. Luck and courage were to waft him to victories despite recklessness, disobedience, and neglect. Not for years—not until he reached a scrap of land by the Little Big Horn—did luck momentarily desert him. Courage never did. Danger was his blind spot.

On June 27, 1863, ten days after Aldie, George Custer rode into headquarters and was greeted as "general."

"Laugh all you please," he retorted, blue eyes flashing. "I'll be a general before this war is over."

A familiar boast. Strangely, his comrades did not rib him. They saluted him smartly.

In his tent was an envelope. It contained his commission as brigadier general of volunteers, giving him command of the 2nd Brigade of the Third Division.

With the engagement at Aldie the nearest thing to a battle in which he had led troops, George Armstrong Custer had vaulted to the command of a brigade! A general at twenty-three! From first lieutenant he had soared past four grades—captain, major, lieutenant colonel, and colonel—above the heads of older, more seasoned officers.

The how and why of his lightning promotion have never been established, though "politics" and "favoritism" are the commonly mouthed explanations. However he got it, one fact was clear to George Custer. Glory, for which he hungered all his life, was nearer his as a commanding officer than as a first lieutenant.

The new general took over his brigade at Hanover, Pennsylvania. He promptly snapped every inch of slackness out of his officers and troopers.

The same youth who had graduated West Point at the bottom of his class changed overnight into a harsh disciplinarian. Cadet Custer, who got demerits for "sitting down on sentry duty," "visiting out of hours," "room unswept," and "tablecloth dirty," became General Custer, a stickler for regulations. The most slovenly dressed male at the Point designed for himself the gaudiest (and most irregular) uniform in the service—black velveteen jacket and trousers, scarlet cravat, blue shirt, and showy gold braid everywhere.

Under his iron rule, the troopers approached mutiny. Then the Boy General took them out to battle. He quieted their protests by his own frightening valor. In any charge, he galloped several lengths before his men, riding like "a circus rider gone mad." He never won their love, but always rewon their respect.

His luck held and he gathered glory. Pursuing Lee from Richmond in the last month of the war, his horsemen hung close to the Confederates' bleeding sides. Custer clawed day and night. He was performing in the front of the stage, and a nation was watching him speed the final curtain.

At Appomattox, luck singled him out. General Longstreet's flag of truce —a crash towel—was delivered into his hands. The Boy General was overjoyed. And yet . . .

Tirelessly he had wooed glory, the handmaiden of war. Now the war was concluding, and he, the youngest major general, was but twenty-five, restless, ambitious. In peace, the soldier's roads to fame become overgrown.

~§

ONE LAST ROAD there was, though it be a dead end. On June 8, 1865, one hundred thousand men swung into Pennsylvania Avenue and paraded toward the reviewing stand in front of the White House.

The Union's Grand Review of victory. The sidewalks overflowed. Men, women, and children screamed their cheers. Wreaths of flowers were draped around the veterans in their neat, faded uniforms.

In the fore of his division rode Custer, magnificently dressed. His beautiful steed, Don Juan, shied before the wildly cheering throng. Custer, the superb horseman, controlled him.

The reviewing stand was just ahead now. The President and his Cabinet were there. Grant was there. Diplomats of many countries were there. What soldier was not glad to share their acclaim? Who dared try for individual attention in the company of a hundred thousand heroes?

Alas, Don Juan bolted. Custer's sombrero flew off. Yellow curls loosed in the wind, he raced past the grandstand. Men shouted and pointed as he finally pulled Don Juan to obedience.

Back in place, sternly riding at the head of his men, the Boy General passed the grandstand again. Men spoke his name, and Grant leaned toward the President's ear. What chance for notice the moment held, George Custer had plucked.

The dead end had been reached. The Confederates were beaten. Where to find the tingling shock of combat, the fame that heats the blood?

In the West the hostile Indians menaced the invading white man. To the West rode Custer of the yellow curls.

At the Little Big Horn, he rashly led 264 men to their doom, and in the heroic drama of defeat wrested for one man immortal glory.

GEORGE ARMSTRONG CUSTER

BORN: New Rumley, Ohio, December 5, 1839.
DIED: Little Big Horn, Montana Territory, June 25, 1876.

THE ILLUSTRATION, PAGE 93: *Union Cavalry men in full charge.*

Joseph Eggleston Johnston
General, Confederate States of America

22

SECOND-BEST GENERAL

SENATOR WILLIAM L. YANCEY of Alabama called for more champagne and proposed a toast.

"Gentlemen, let us drink to the only man who can save the Confederacy—General Joseph E. Johnston!"

The room in Griffin's Restaurant in Richmond rang with cries of "Hear! Hear!" The applause died slowly. The men resumed their seats as General Johnston, a dapper, bright-eyed man of fifty-four, stood up.

He lifted his glass.

"Mr. Yancey," he said seriously, "the man you describe is now in the field, in the person of General Robert E. Lee. I will drink to his health!"

Yancey sprang to his feet and quickly said, "Your modesty is equaled only by your valor."

Johnston's valor was unquestioned. And his many wounds—in Mexico in 1847 and on the Virginia Peninsula earlier that year of 1862—attested to his nearness to the firing.

But it was his fate to serve the same

cause as the superb Robert E. Lee. Had there been no Lee, Joseph Johnston might today be acclaimed the favorite son of the Confederacy. Instead, he is its neglected general.

The Johnston role of second best had begun a generation back. Peter Johnston, Joseph's father, served in the Revolutionary War under Robert's father, General "Light-Horse Harry" Lee, Washington's artillery chief.

At West Point Robert graduated second in the class of 1829 in which Joseph stood thirteenth. In the Mexican War, the uneven contest was continued.

Johnston was wounded five times. "He is a great soldier," declared the commanding officer, General Winfield Scott. "But he has an unfortunate knack of getting himself shot in nearly every engagement."

At the same time, Scott termed Lee's two trips across the lava bed known as the *pedregal* "the greatest feat of physical and moral courage performed by any individual in my knowledge . . ."

In 1855 Johnston had attained the rank of lieutenant colonel in the First Cavalry. Lee was lieutenant colonel of the 2nd Cavalry. Five years later Johnston was appointed Quartermaster General of the Army, and elevated to brig-

adier general. For the first and only time he outranked Lee.

With the fall of Fort Sumter, Johnston resigned from the United States Army to cast his destiny with that of his native state, Virginia. Governor Letcher commissioned him a major general of the state forces.

Two weeks later Johnston was reduced to brigadier general. By some vague policy, there could only be one major general of Virginia. The honor belonged to Lee, who had been given his rank five days earlier.

When the Confederacy issued commissions, Johnston immediately became a brigadier. Lee held back; he was unwilling to leave the Virginia forces until their official transfer to the national army. Then President Davis appointed Lee his military adviser. Johnston was sent into the field.

At Manassas (Bull Run), Johnston assumed command over Beauregard as senior brigadier. During the battle, Colonel Thomas Jackson stood like "a stone wall," and Colonel Jubal Early delivered the decisive blow. Brigadier General Johnston won the first victory of the war for the South.

Early in September, 1861, Congress confirmed appointments for the rank of full general. As a former brigadier in the United States Army, Johnston considered himself the top officer in the Confederacy. His promotion was dated as of July 4, 1861, dropping him in seniority to fourth. Dated earlier were the commissions of Samuel Cooper, A. S. Johnston, and Lee. Johnston was enraged at the list.

In a fit of temper he wrote a letter to President Davis. Davis replied curtly. Johnston's arguments he classed as "unbecoming" and "unfounded."

The subject was slammed closed. But the ill feeling remained throughout the war, hurting Johnston gravely.

In the spring of 1862, General George McClellan led his huge Northern Army of the Potomac up the Peninsula toward Richmond. Johnston, commanding the Confederate forces in northern Virginia, retreated cautiously.

At Seven Pines (Fair Oaks), he fought his only major attacking action. An exploding shell wounded him in the chest. Lee replaced him, with the bluecoats but seven miles from Richmond. Lee's brilliant thrusts forced McClellan to abandon his campaign for keeps.

By November Johnston had recovered enough to resume command. But Lee had risen as the brightest star of the Confederacy. Johnston was assigned to the Western theater.

Friends gave him a farewell party at Griffin's Restaurant on the eve of his departure. Senator Yancey offered the toast, and Johnston replied:

"The man you describe is now in the field, in the person of General Robert E. Lee."

With what bitter coin did Joseph Johnston pay that tribute!

In the West he glumly took charge of Bragg's army in Tennessee and Pemberton's army in Mississippi. In May, 1863, he was unable to cope with President Davis's nagging and the heavily superior Northern forces. He yielded Vicksburg to Grant.

In the spring of 1864 he met the combined Northern armies under William T. Sherman. Johnston retreated, striving to keep his outnumbered army intact. Whenever Sherman made a mistake, as at Kenesaw Mountain, Johnston uncurled and struck. Nonetheless, the Confederates were pushed back to Atlanta.

For his lack of aggressiveness he was removed by President Davis. Offense-minded John Hood replaced him. Hood slaughtered most of his army with futile attacks.

In review, Johnston seems overly cautious. His retreating tactics brought him the semi-humorous reputation as "the general who never lost a battle."

How good was he?

When replaced by a general of thoughtful daring, like Lee, he appears timid and without confidence. When replaced by a general of reckless daring, like Hood, he appears wise and prudent. Always, he was steady, calm, and allergic to risk.

As the Confederacy splintered, Johnston was recalled to a brief period of active duty. He patched together a force known as the Army of Tennessee. For two months he contested the path of Sherman's steam roller. He surrendered at Durham Station, North Carolina, April 26, 1865, seventeen days after Lee.

Ironically, he was outshone by Lee even in defeat.

Today Appomattox Courthouse, the village where Lee surrendered to Grant, is a name emblazoned in American lore.

Durham Station is but a speck on a road map.

❦❦❦•❦❦❦

JOSEPH EGGLESTON JOHNSTON

BORN: Prince Edward County, Virginia, February 3, 1807.
DIED: Washington, D. C., March 21, 1891.

THE ILLUSTRATION, PAGE 97: *Two Confederate bullet molds for casting lead bullets, with the Enfield rifle supplied to the South by British blockade runners.*

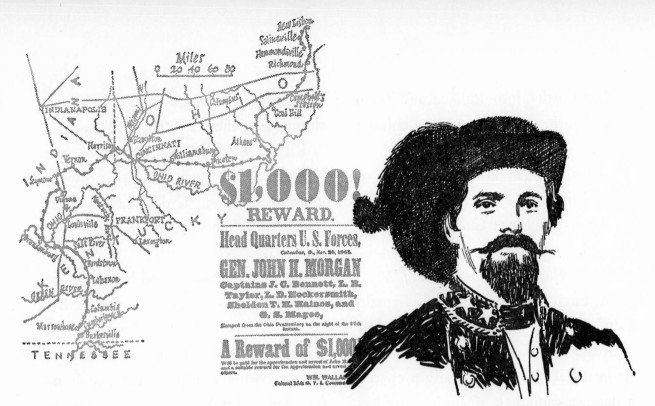

John Hunt Morgan

Brigadier General, Confederate States of America

23

PRINCE OF RAIDERS

"I TELL YOU, Morgan's coming!" In the summer of 1863, that cry startled Midwestern towns. General John Morgan was raiding again, farther north than ever. He had come bucketing up from Kentucky with 2,460 raiders and four pieces of artillery. Communities hitherto presumed safe from shooting suddenly quaked under the hoofs of invasion.

On July 2, Morgan and his 2nd Kentucky Cavalry had ridden out of Burkesville with orders to lure off the Yankees. Braxton Bragg, commanding the Con-federate Army in the West, wanted a decoy while he retreated from Tullahoma to Chattanooga.

Once under way, Morgan yielded to a heady temptation. To give Bragg more time, he disobeyed orders by leaving Kentucky. He and his men crossed the Ohio River, stole horses, tore up tracks, burned bridges, and plundered whatever they needed.

Resistance spouted along his route. Not only did the regular Yank cavalry pursue, but the state militia turned out by the tens of thousands. Farther and farther north—into Indiana and Ohio —the panting, dwindling Gray column raced.

"John Morgan is still in Ohio, or rather is in Ohio without being allowed to be still," the Chicago *Tribune* gloated.

"I tell you, Morgan's coming!"

In East Liverpool, Ohio, Captain Edwin Burbick heard the warning while at breakfast. As commander of the militia in the area, he had already prepared a defense should the feared Confederate show up. It was a faultless scheme— in Burbick's mind.

As he fumbled on his saber the front door banged open. A tall man with cold, grayish-blue eyes strode in.

There could be no question of the intruder's identity. It was General Morgan himself, though his blue plaid jacket bore no insignia of rank. The dust of three states coated his cavalry boots and gray pants. His broad shoulders sagged with a terrible weariness.

"Captain Burbick?" he demanded. Without pausing for a reply, he said, "I promise you that no property in your district will be damaged. In return, you guide us to the Pennsylvania border."

Burbick's fine plan went scat, and he agreed. Outside were all that remained of Morgan's hit-and-run roughriders.

Three hundred tough and reckless men slumped in their saddles, exhausted.

Riding out of East Liverpool, the sharp-eyed Morgan spied a growing column of dust. Union cavalry had flanked him and were knifing in for the kill.

The game was up, and hastily Morgan tried to salvage what he could. "If I surrender to you, Captain Burbick, will you grant my own terms?" he asked.

John Morgan his prisoner! The dumfounded militiaman recovered enough to stammer. "Y-yes, certainly."

Morgan's conditions were: paroles for every raider; each man to keep his horse, and in the case of an officer, his arms. Burbick happily agreed to everything. So died in hurried bargaining the raid that had terrified the North for three weeks.

The 9th Kentucky Cavalry galloped up shortly after the surrender. Its commanding officer refused to honor the conditions Burbick had so willingly allowed. Morgan and what was left of his division were taken to Cincinnati in triumph.

The citizenry was in an ugly mood. An armed mob of several thousand met the raiders at the railroad station. Men waved pistols and chanted, "Hang the cutthroats!"

Newspapers denounced the daredevils who had committed the outrage of gutting sacred land—*Northern* land. Vexed by the success of the raid, reporters played up its disastrous ending.

True, Morgan had lost heavily in men and horses. But even the vengeful Chicago *Tribune* conceded: "The capture of the raiders releases to other duties five times their number of Federal troops who have been engrossed in the business of catching them."

THE NORTH was determined to make an example of Morgan. He had been a thorn in its side too long. He and his raiders ought to have been put in a regular prisoner camp. Instead, they were locked in the Ohio penitentiary at Columbus. Inside the grim concrete structure, they were treated like common criminals.

They protested to the governor. Eventually he took heed and improved their lot. One of the improvements was to gain Morgan his freedom.

The Union military commander at Columbus told the prison authorities he would replace their guards with soldiers during the day. At night the regular prison guards would resume their duties.

As a result, the prison guards ceased to inspect the cells. The civilian authorities, disgusted at all the fuss, decided to let the raiders keep their cells clean or live in filth.

The last inspection of the cells was made November 4. That same night Morgan began tunneling to freedom.

On November 27 a guard noticed a rope fashioned of bedclothes hanging from the outer wall of the prison. Morgan and six of his captains had escaped.

The raiders had emerged at daybreak. They had come out into the cold rain like figures from the past.

Seven months they had been imprisoned. In that period Confederate fortunes had begun to topple. Fighting had lost the swords-and-roses chivalry of the early days. War had reached beyond the armies into the fields and corncribs and factories.

This new, total war had passed the stage where it could be won by saber swinging. Men like John Morgan, who fought off to the side of the main battles, might briefly thrill the South and lift morale. They could no longer hope to win by gallant, old-fashioned cavalry sweeps.

In April, 1864, Morgan was given command of the Department of South-west Virginia. He tried to organize a standing force like his old 2nd Kentucky Cavalry. But discipline had vanished. Most of his original troopers were either captives or dead. These new men mainly were lawless and loot-hungry.

On September 3, 1864, Morgan moved to attack Union detachments near Knoxville, Tennessee. While camped overnight in Greenville, enemy troops slipped through his slipshod pickets.

The Yanks surrounded the house where he slept. In the morning they called upon him to surrender. The Prince of Raiders was slain trying to sneak away.

⋘⋙•⋘⋙•⋘⋙•⋘⋙•⋘⋙

JOHN HUNT MORGAN

BORN: Huntsville, Alabama, June 1, 1825.
DIED: Greenville, Tennessee, September 4, 1864.

THE ILLUSTRATION, PAGE 101: *Map of Morgan's raid through Kentucky, Indiana and Ohio, with a poster offering reward for the capture of Morgan.*

Belle Boyd
Spy, Confederate States of America

24

GIRL SPY

IN THE LITTLE Virginia town of Martinsburg, the Fourth of July, 1861, was celebrated by Union soldiers with the explosive help of one hundred and fifty barrels of captured whisky.

Bands played national airs and regiments paraded. The whisky flowed, and toward evening men roamed the streets, ignoring their officers. Rifles were discharged. Windows were broken and houses entered.

Among the homes looted was Ben Boyd's. Ben himself was off fighting for the South, a volunteer private of forty-

four years. But his wife and teen-age daughter Belle were home. The blue-coats grew ugly when they learned Belle had her bedroom decorated with Confederate flags.

Belle's maid sneaked upstairs and swiftly destroyed the flags. Thwarted, the Yanks resolved to fly the Stars and Stripes over the Boyd roof.

At this point Mrs. Boyd had all she could take. She had stoically witnessed her home being plundered; she refused, however, to submit to this final humiliation. Quietly but firmly she announced that every member of her household would die rather than see "that flag" flown over them.

One of the soldiers retorted in violent language and threatening gestures. Frightened for her mother, the seventeen-year-old Belle drew a pistol and shot the Yankee.

The dying man was carried outside. Some of his comrades loitered by the porch, darkly vengeful. Belle sent to Federal headquarters for aid. It arrived in time to save the house from being put to the torch.

An investigation by Union officers cleared Belle of murder. But she was henceforth regarded as highly dangerous. The Boyd home was placed under guard.

This only inflamed the girl, and she began to work secretly for the South. The guards outside her house and the officers who often visited in the parlor were listened to very, very attentively.

Although not a beauty, Belle had definite allure. She had been well educated and was an accomplished pianist, horsewoman, and dancer. She relied on her wit, feminine charm, and excellent figure to assist her ears. Few soldiers, after a while in her company, suspected they faced an accomplished foe.

Bits and pieces fell from careless lips.

Belle's nimble mind sifted everything. She gathered much knowledge concerning the position, movement, and strength of Union forces in the area. This information she wrote down and had one of her faithful slaves deliver to Confederate leaders, often to Stonewall Jackson or Jeb Stuart.

For a while all went smoothly. Then a message was intercepted. A wrathful colonel read Belle an Article of War. It stated that anyone abetting enemies of the United States Government might suffer death.

Belle hid behind her tender years. Was her offense as serious as all that? She escaped with a reprimand.

For the next few days she switched to stealing Union arms and ammunition, which she smuggled into Southern lines. Later, in July, she joined the hospital staff at Front Royal and tended the wounded brought in from Manassas (Bull Run). She soon longed for a more vigorous role than nursing.

What she wanted she usually got. By October she was a courier riding between Generals Beauregard and Jackson and their officers. Here was a challenge to test her mettle. She proved more than equal to the demands—both in bravery and in the elegance of her perfumed riding habit. Tales of romantic adventure blossomed around the fashionable young horsewoman. Within weeks she seemed more imaginary than real.

FOR ALL HER derring-do as a night rider, Belle's most important contribution to the Confederate Army occurred one day during Stonewall Jackson's Shenandoah Valley campaign. She signaled Jackson's forces from Front Royal that by haste they could cross the bridge which the Federals intended to burn. Thus Jackson could save a route for an attack on Union General Banks.

Belle braved Northern ball and shell to race out to the advancing skirmishers. Whether her intelligence was new to Jackson or merely confirmed what he already knew is not certain. Whichever, he was grateful.

I thank you, for myself and for the army, for the immense service you have rendered your country, he wrote her.

When the North captured Front Royal in July, 1862, Belle was arrested and brought to Washington. So celebrated was she that on one leg of the journey four hundred and fifty cavalrymen guarded the carriage containing the slender, eighteen-year-old girl!

Belle was imprisoned in the Old Capitol Prison. The Northern press took petty revenge of the defenseless captive. They belittled her looks and minimized her value. The Washington *Star* assured its readers that the "notorious female spy" is disappointingly thin, poorly educated, and talkative—altogether a coarse adventuress. *Leslie's Weekly* crowed that "Belle Boyd, the Secesh Cleopatra, is caged at last."

Belle was released after a month as a part of an official exchange. In August, 1863, she was again arrested and confined in Carroll prison, Washington, until December 1. After touring the South, she sailed in the spring for England. She carried letters from Jefferson Davis to Confederate agents and sympathizers abroad.

Her ship was captured by a United States man-of-war, and Belle was made prisoner once more. But she reached England unhampered, having won the love of Lieutenant Samuel Hardinge, who had been put in command of the prize ship. Renouncing the Union for Belle, Hardinge married her in England, the first of her three husbands.

Two volumes of memoirs, *Belle Boyd in Camp and Prison*, were published in London in 1865. After the war, she stayed in England and ventured onto the stage. She enjoyed success and continued her acting career in America. She retired in 1869 to wed a second time.

In 1885 her fortunes declined, and she turned to giving dramatic recitals of her adventures as a Confederate agent. She delivered her narrative, entitled "North and South, or the Perils of a Spy," smartly uniformed in Confederate gray and a plumed cavalry hat.

It was during one of these performances that she died of a heart attack in Kilbourne (now Wisconsin Dells), Wisconsin. She was buried there under the inscription:

> BELLE BOYD
> Confederate Spy
> Born in Virginia
> ————
> Erected By a Comrade

BELLE BOYD

> BORN: Martinsburg, Virginia, May 9, 1843.
> DIED: Kilbourne, Wisconsin, June 11, 1900.

THE ILLUSTRATION, PAGE 105: *The spy passes on her information.*

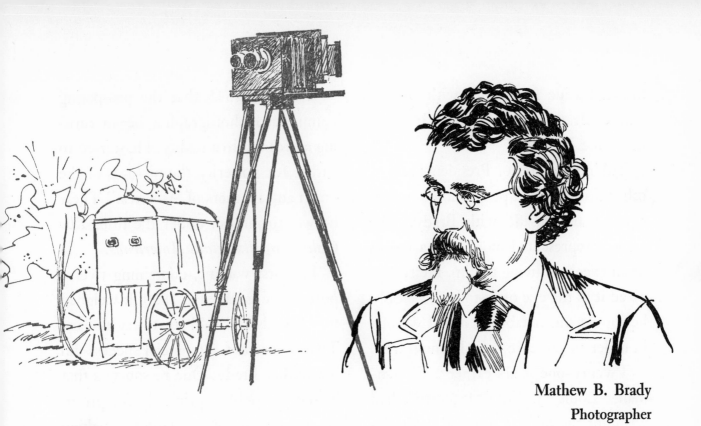

Mathew B. Brady
Photographer

25

BATTLEFIELD CAMERAMAN

THE UNITED STATES was not yet a house divided when a tall, smooth-shaven man arrived in New York City. A former Congressman, he had fair reason to hope for his party's Vice Presidential nomination. So it was natural that he went to Broadway and Tenth Street to have his portrait taken by Mathew Brady.

Brady stood him before the camera, propped a book under his hand, and stepped back critically. No, the tall man looked stiff, self-conscious. Brady got his subject to relax, and the shutter clicked. The result was a three-quarter-length portrait of quiet strength and beauty. Wood engravings of the picture appeared in newspapers, and lithographs copied from it were sold by Currier and Ives.

Two days later, on February 27, 1860, the tall man spoke at Cooper Institute. The speech, along with the dignity of Brady's widely circulated portrait, convinced the people that the gangling ex-rail splitter was a man worthy of public trust.

Mathew Brady fondly remembered his next meeting with Abraham Lincoln —in the White House. The President

109

brushed aside formalities with the remark, "Brady and the Cooper Institute made me President."

Taking pictures of Presidents and of other distinguished people amounted to a one-man crusade with Brady. The camera represented more than a means of an excellent living to him. He recognized it as the eye of history. Tirelessly he sought out notable men and women in order to preserve their likenesses.

Twenty-one years earlier a Frenchman, Louis J. M. Daguerre, had wrought the miracle. He had devised a method of "taking on copper the exact resemblance of scenes and living objects." That was the same summer in which Mathew Brady, a restless farm boy of sixteen, arrived in New York City.

A year later Mathew enrolled at America's first school of photography. He paid the handsome sum of fifty dollars to Professor Samuel Morse (later to invent the telegraph) to learn how to take and develop daguerreotypes.

Inside of three years the youth was operating his own portrait studio. His work lifted him above his competitors, and soon thousands were patronizing the "only Brady." At every national and international contest he entered, his daguerreotypes carried off first prize.

It was in 1845 that the prospering commercial photographer began turning a dream into a reality. He started to gather for posterity the pictures of the "men and mothers of America." These he was to publish under the title, *The Gallery of Illustrious Americans.*

The first volume, containing twelve portraits, was issued in 1850. It weighed five pounds and sold for thirty dollars. That it was not a financial success did not bother Brady. One reason was that he did not publish primarily for profit. A second reason was the money-making "wet plate process," newly introduced from England.

The new method, which fixed pictures on glass, allowed for unlimited reproductions, and in all respects surpassed the daguerreotype. It boomed business enormously. The rage for expensive "imperials," or life-size portraits, was followed by the equally profitable craze for cheap *carte de visite,* a small cardboard bearing the photograph of the caller. These were run off by the millions.

Then war came. Brady forsook his two luxurious galleries in New York City and Washington. He felt he must do his part.

"A spirit in my feet cried, 'Go,' and I went," he recalled.

The War Department was concerned with winning battles, not with photographing them. Finally he was granted a card that bore two words, "Pass Brady." He might photograph the Union armies if he did not make a nuisance of himself. And if he paid his own expenses.

The conditions did not discourage him. History was marching. Its image must not sweep past unrecorded.

Soon a slight man with a pointed beard and thick, blue-tinted spectacles became a regular fixture in camp and field. Instead of a uniform he wore a linen duster and flat straw hat. He carried no weapons, only a camera. His equipment-ladened wagon looked like nothing ever seen on wheels. The soldiers jokingly called it a "What-is-it wagon," and the nickname stuck.

&

FOR ALL their strangeness, Brady and his twenty-two teams of assistants amazed battle-hardened veterans with their willingness to rush to the firing. Braving dangers, however, was but a small part of it. The handicaps before and after the "click" would probably drive most photographers today into another profession.

Over rutted roads and uncleared ground Brady and his men moved their fragile glass plates, chemicals, and awkward light-proof developing tents. Before taking a picture, the plate (usually 8 x 10 inches) was coated with collodion, a highly sensitive solution. This had to be done with great care. A stray breath or waft of hot air would result in a blank area. After the plate was exposed, it ordinarily had to be developed within five minutes.

Every phase of army life in the North was recorded on some thirty-five hundred wet plates. Brady succeeded in fulfilling his stupendous dream of photographing the war. In doing so, he ruined himself. When the last rifle was lowered, his fortune of one hundred thousand dollars was wiped out.

Over the years he repaid his debts—by remaining at the camera despite rheumatism and ever-weakening eyes. The lavish studios and the legion of bustling assistants belonged to yesteryear. He worked now above the Pennsylvania Railroad ticket office in Washington. The pioneering torch had passed to younger men, many of whom had learned their art under the old master.

Misfortune dogged his last years. After being seriously injured by a horsecar, he was cared for by friends in New

York City. With their backing, he hopefully laid plans for a grand exhibition of his war scenes. The showing was to restore his wealth and prestige. But five days before opening night, he breathed his last.

In his room were found a battered satchel and some old clothing.

There were also two objects of value, more sentimental than real: an ivory-handled cane and a ring, both given him by the Prince of Wales during his heyday as a photographer.

He died, then, a poor man. Yet he left a priceless treasure—his photographs.

Because of Mathew Brady, Americans may today *look* at their past: at Mrs. Alexander Hamilton and at President John Quincy Adams, at Mark Twain and at General Tom Thumb, at the ruins of Richmond and at the dead of Gettysburg.

<hr />

MATHEW B. BRADY

BORN: Warren County, New York, 1823.
DIED: New York City, New York, January 15, 1896.

THE ILLUSTRATION, PAGE 109: *Brady's 'What-Is-It' Wagon with Camera. (Courtesy, George Eastman House, Rochester, New York.)*

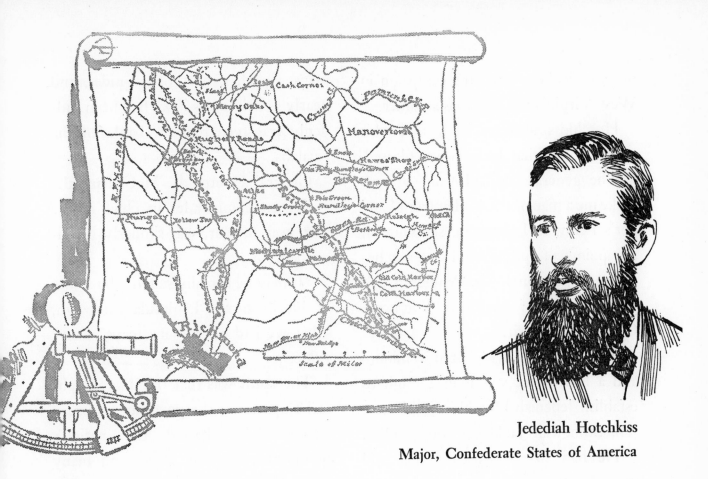

Jedediah Hotchkiss
Major, Confederate States of America

26

THE PATHFINDER

JED HOTCHKISS read the message with immediate disbelief. Either it was a mistake or someone's prank.

There was no reason for Stonewall Jackson to want to see him. Why would the most talked about general in the army bother with the acting adjutant of the militia regiment from Augusta County, Virginia?

Yet the message said: *General T. J. Jackson wishes to see Jedediah Hotchkiss...*

His comrades assured him that the message was genuine. Behind his back they agreed there must be another Jedediah Hotchkiss, improbable as *that* might be.

Hotchkiss stuck to his conviction that the whole affair was a hoax—until the morning of March 26, 1862, when he faced the general.

Jackson scrutinized him for a long moment. Then he demanded to know whether Hotchkiss had drawn the

113

maps of Robert Garnett's campaign in West Virginia the previous summer.

Hotchkiss admitted he had. To his relief, he saw that Jackson was pleased.

The general said: "I want you to make me a map of the Valley from Harper's Ferry to Lexington, showing all the points of offense and defense between those points. Mr. Pendleton will give you orders for whatever you need. Good morning, sir."

The interview had lasted a minute and a half. That was long enough to establish Jedediah Hotchkiss in his new job, Stonewall Jackson's topographer.

He had to start with gullies and mounds. There were no detailed maps of the Shenandoah Valley, or, for that matter, of any locality in Virginia. Only one map of the state existed. Its scale, five miles to the inch, made it unsatisfactory for military uses.

The North was hardly better off. But fighting on home ground, the Southerners ought to have enjoyed the advantage of knowing the terrain. They did not.

This ignorance was pointed up by General Richard Taylor. "The Confederate commanders," said Taylor, "knew no more about the topography of the country than they did about Central Africa. We were profoundly ignorant of the country, were without maps, sketches, or proper guides, and nearly as helpless as if we had been suddenly transferred to the banks of the Lualaba."

General George B. McClellan, the Northern commander in chief in the first year of war, was similarly handicapped.

"It may be broadly stated," he wrote of his ill-starred Peninsula campaign, "that we had no military maps of any value."

The truth was that the Topographical Engineers—the governmental map agency—had charted the nation's boundaries, the Far West, and many other regions. But the South, from the Atlantic coastline to Texas, had been omitted.

Both sides had to rely upon scouts and spies, who were often untrustworthy. Not until 1864 did a satisfactory number of maps reach the field commanders.

There was, however, one commander who never fumbled because a scout forgot which way a road turned. Stonewall Jackson had the Hotchkiss survey of the Shenandoah Valley. Armed with those accurate drawings, Jackson was able to move surely. His brilliant Valley campaign of the spring of 1862 was the consequence.

Old Jack's soldiers marveled at his touch. "He knew every hole and corner of the Valley as if he had made it himself," declared a sergeant.

The praise was, unwittingly, paid to Hotchkiss, a transplanted Yankee. Born in Windsor, New York, he had discovered the charm of Virginia while on a walking tour at nineteen. Settling in Augusta County, he had opened an academy. As a hobby he drew maps.

Hotchkiss had only to ride over a stretch of countryside once to have its features imprinted on his mind. His trained eye and rapid pencil were in constant demand by Jackson.

"I often made rough sketches for the general on the march or during engagements, in answer to his requests for information," Hotchkiss remembered.

A carefully prepared map sometimes had too much detail of a nonmilitary nature. While Jackson watched, Hotchkiss would sketch a particular point from memory, using colored pencils for emphasis.

Shortages of pencils, pens, ink and other elementary supplies were forever causing Hotchkiss grief. Two hundred yards of tracing paper captured from the Federals in July, 1862, was cause for celebration.

THE SCARCITIES became progressively more acute. Early in 1863 a Southern purchasing agent went to England. He sent back chemicals, triangles, rules, T-squares, tracing cloth, pantographs, pens, pencils, water colors, and drawing paper. The shipments, threading the blockade, relieved the shortages, though not for long. Hotchkiss and the other Confederate topographers were soon back to ferreting among captured Yankee stores.

Jackson made wide use of the "Professor," as Hotchkiss was nicknamed. Because of his remarkable sense of direction, Hotchkiss was often employed to bring up a column at night, or to guide a unit into position across unfamiliar ground. Moreover, Hotchkiss's unerring eye made him a sort of super scout. He could ascertain swiftly the best routes for an advance.

Finding byways and hidden roads developed into his specialty. At Chancellorsville, Virginia, that specialty contributed to the Confederates' most spectacular victory. It also brought the tragic loss of Jackson.

For it was Hotchkiss who discovered that a road had been privately opened through a forest for the transport of cordwood and iron ore. It led around the right flank of the Union army, now commanded by General Joseph Hooker. Down that secret road marched Jackson, to victory and death.

Jed Hotchkiss continued in the Army of Northern Virginia, attaining the rank of major. In 1864 he opened a topographical office in Staunton, Virginia, employing two assistants. The same year he served Jubal Early, Jackson's successor in the Shenandoah Valley.

Despite the shortages of materials, his war maps compare well with the very best of the lavishly equipped Union engineers. Of the 1,006 maps in the *Official Records Atlas*, 202 are by Confederates; of these, more than half are by Hotchkiss.

Most of the drawings are those he rendered for Stonewall Jackson. When the famous foot cavalry marched, it was with Stonewall's brain and courage, but the eyes of the "Professor."

To Jed Hotchkiss, unsung hero with a pencil, must go a small but essential portion of the credit for that most wonderful of all campaigns—Jackson in the Valley.

JEDEDIAH HOTCHKISS

BORN: Windsor, New York, 1847 (?).
DIED: 1908 (?).

THE ILLUSTRATION, PAGE 113: *A Hotchkiss map with sextant.*

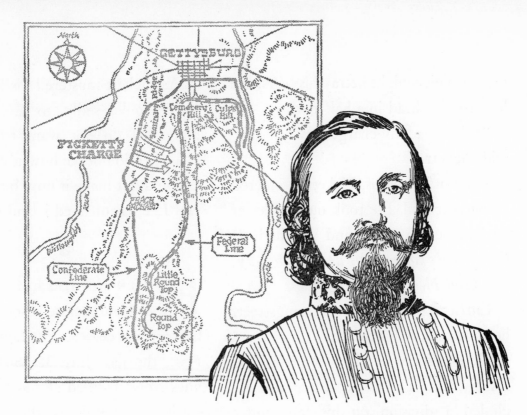

George Edward Pickett
Major General, Confederate States of America

27

PICKETT'S CHARGE

SHORTLY BEFORE three in the afternoon the Confederate artillery barrage ceased. Except for a few scattered guns, a strange quiet rolled across the battlefield at Gettysburg.

General George Pickett sat composing a love letter. The day was hot, approaching ninety degrees, and humid. Pickett's ringlets had uncurled and his hair drooped upon his shoulders. The perfume with which he anointed his head and beard had evaporated in two days of hard fighting.

A dispatch arrived from Colonel E. Porter Alexander of the artillery. It read:

If you are to advance at all, you must come at once, or we will not be able to support you.

Pickett took the warning to his brooding corps commander, defense-minded James "Old Pete" Longstreet.

"General," said Pickett. "Shall I advance?"

Longstreet did not reply. He dared

not; his voice might betray his fears. He lowered his head in a half nod.

"I shall lead my charge forward, sir," said Pickett.

After a few paces, Pickett wondered about that nod. He took out the letter he had been writing and penciled: *If Old Peter's nod means death, good-by, and God bless you, little one!*

Entrusting the letter to Longstreet, he rode back to his men.

He had forty-five hundred troops in his division. The assault force also included a division on his left under James Pettigrew, as well as two brigades under Alfred Scales and James Lane. All in all, approximately eleven thousand men under George Edward Pickett.

The plan was admirably simple. Pickett, who had graduated last in his class at West Point, understood it thoroughly. He had to advance from a crest, merge with Pettigrew, and move to where six thousand Federals crouched behind a stone wall and earthworks, fourteen hundred yards away on Cemetery Ridge.

The Federal artillery in the sector was quiet. Apparently it had been quelled by nearly two hours of concentrated cannonading from one hundred and forty Confederate pieces.

As Pickett mustered his lines, Longstreet spoke sadly to Colonel Alexander. "I do not want to make this charge. I do not see how it can succeed. I would not make it now but that General Lee has ordered it and expects it."

≈§

FIFTEEN MINUTES had elapsed since the Confederate "softening up" barrage had ceased. The hour was 3:10 P.M., the day July 3, 1863. Pickett's lines stood formed at the bottom of a swale out of sight of the enemy. The speeches were over. The order sounded:

"Forward—guide center—*march!*"

Out stepped the ten color-bearers of the leading line. As though on dress parade the men walked shoulder to shoulder up the rise.

The front sprang into the sight of the Yanks abruptly and wonderfully, like a row of cardboard soldiers bouncing upright in a shooting gallery. Within five minutes all Pickett's men were past the crest, and Pettigrew's men were out of the woods. The Yanks had a panoramic view of the entire force advancing on them under artillery cover.

Pickett's three brigades came on in two main lines, spaced one hundred yards apart, and Pettigrew's in three lines. They moved without noise, covering the ground at a steady gait, closing a hundred yards almost every minute.

After traveling four hundred and fifty yards, Pickett, sixty feet in the rear, gave the command, "Left oblique!" Every soldier swerved forty-five degrees to his left. The whole division swiveled toward Pettigrew's with the precision of a machine.

Eight minutes after stepping off, the front line reached a hollow about midway between the two armies. Out of sight, and well protected from fire, the division re-formed. In the last few hundred feet, Union artillery had begun to fray the picture-book formation. Nonetheless, morale ran high.

Up from the hollow the division marched on command. Another seven hundred feet and the left side contacted Pettigrew's right. Now the two divisions showed a solid front, three quarters of a mile wide. The advance funneled into a direct, one-column assault against the Federal line, four hundred yards away.

All at once, the Union artillery in the line of march roared out. It had not been quelled by the Confederate cannonade. The Yanks had just quit to save ammunition, and the infantry was what they had saved for. Canister, the shrapnel type of shot used at close range, burst against the splendid, on-coming human tide.

Officers toppled from dying horses. File closers chased play outs and cursed them back into ranks. Everywhere men pitched to the ground. The survivors stooped forward, as if bucking a furious wind. White-faced lieutenants shouted, "Steady, boys!" "Close up! Close up!" "Don't fire yet!" "Close up!"

The Yankees licked their lips and tightened their fingers on their triggers. "Don't fire until you're told, men!" "Lie low!" officers called, eyes on the riddled Gray column.

The bluecoats gazed spellbound. "Remember, fire low!" The old warning rang shrilly from throats gone dry. "Fire low—*fire!*"

George Pickett heard the thunderous crash of that first volley from the Gordi farmhouse, three hundred yards in the rear. After all, a commanding general was not supposed to join the first wave of an assault. . . .

The bleeding Gray column reeled, recovered, and stormed into the Union muzzles. Face to face, the two lines loaded and fired, loaded and fired. Nobody expected to come out of that patch of hell alive.

Somehow the Confederates punched through in three places. They held a clump of trees for two minutes, fighting with shot, fists, and rocks. A push by reinforcements from behind would win the day, and very likely the war. But behind were only the dead and wounded for half a mile.

The Union forces rallied. The Southerners, what remained of them, fell back. Twenty minutes after it began, Pickett's charge—the "high-water mark" of the war—had passed to the poets and historians.

Three quarters of Pickett's division had fallen, including every field officer except one. General Lee rode among the survivors. "My fault! My fault!" he repeated in a tone of agony.

Pickett himself had retreated unscratched from the farmhouse before his men were repulsed. Two months later, having maintained excellent health, he wed his sweetheart. He was not dismissed from the army until the last days of the war.

❧❧❧•❧❧❧

GEORGE EDWARD PICKETT

BORN: Richmond, Virginia, January 25, 1825.
DIED: Norfolk, Virginia, July 30, 1875.

THE ILLUSTRATION, PAGE 117: *Map of the third day of Battle of Gettysburg showing battle lines at the time of Pickett's charge.*

John Clifford Pemberton
Lieutenant General, Confederate States of America

28

THE GOOD SOLDIER

THE LIVING cried out in fever and thirst, or sobbed in pain. The dying shrieked their fear. The dead rotted silently in the heat of the Mississippi sun.

They lay like that for three days—three thousand Union soldiers sprawled in the no-man's land between the lines.

Being Northern soldiers, they were the responsibility of U. S. Grant. Here at Vicksburg, as at Spottsylvania and Cold Harbor to come, Grant showed an unpleasant side to his stubbornness. He refused to ask for a truce to bury the dead and treat the wounded.

His opponent was not so hard. *In the name of humanity*, wrote John Pemberton on May 25, 1863, *I have the honor to propose a cessation of hostilities for two and a half hours, that you may be able to remove your dead and dying men.*

Grant accepted the Confederate commander's proposal at 6:00 P.M.

The dead and dying had been abandoned after a vain attack on the works

121

protecting Vicksburg. This fruitless charge—the second in three days—was to be Grant's last effort to capture the city by assault.

He now settled down to siege tactics. He would starve out this man Pemberton. Already he had spent eight months pounding the outnumbered Confederates. Pemberton had been outmaneuvered and outhit, and driven back inside Vicksburg.

But Pemberton had not quit.

From a dugout in a bluff two hundred feet above the city, Pemberton gazed down upon the enemy six hundred yards from his lines. Nearly as far as he could see, the mighty Union divisions crouched, menacing him on three sides. On the fourth side, behind, were the Mississippi River and the gunboats of the Union admiral, David D. Porter.

"Hold Vicksburg at all costs," President Davis had ordered. "The city is the nailhead that holds the two halves of the South together."

If Grant yanked that nailhead, the Confederacy was divided; Louisiana, Texas, and Arkansas were shut off from the eastern states. And the Union would have all the Mississippi River besides.

Pemberton, commander of the Department of the Mississippi and East Louisiana, had appealed for reinforcements. Joseph E. Johnston, the commander in chief in the West, held a view opposed to President Davis's. Johnston wanted to save the army by giving up Vicksburg.

Although hampered by the clash between his superiors, Davis and Johnston, and surrounded and outnumbered, Pemberton dug in. With all the skill drawn from thirty years in the Army, he laid out defenses that were to serve as a model to military students in the future.

One day during the first week of the siege, Grant lighted up a cigar and reminisced. He recalled his service with John Pemberton in the Mexican war.

"A more honorable man never lived," he said to his favorite, General William Sherman.

He smoked calmly as his artillery went to work gouging out Pemberton's defenders. The Confederate guns were quiet. Grant knew what that meant.

Pemberton was low on ammunition. His orders were to conserve ammunition. The most acute shortage was in cartridge caps.

On the eleventh day of siege, eighteen thousand caps were smuggled into the lines from General Johnston. But no relief columns marched into sight.

Pemberton was reduced to ingenuity.

He had his ordnance officer collect all the enemy's unexploded Parrott shells. They were transported to Paxton's foundry, recapped, and hurled back at the Yanks.

Grant's guns steadily ate away at the fortifications. The Blue lines tightened. On the thirteenth day, unpleasant tidings reached Pemberton. Grant, inching forward, had closed to within seventy-five yards of the Confederate trenches in places.

The constant bombardment had forced the civilian population to seek refuge in caves about the city. By the thirty-seventh day, the fifth dispatch arrived from Joseph Johnston. Pemberton crumpled the note in his fist.

He was forsaken. Johnston refused to sacrifice two armies in the groundless hope of rescuing one.

⋙

THE SIEGE entered its second month. The men in the trenches sickened from the cramped quarters. The meat gave out, and mule was issued. In their hunger, officers and men thought it "not only nutritious but very palatable and in every way preferable to poor beef."

Grant sat and puffed his cigar. The city's supply of food must be giving out. How long would Pemberton feel honor bound to resist?

By the forty-fifth day John Pemberton faced a forlorn choice. He must surrender or cut his way out. Grant had nibbled to within twenty-five feet of his lines. A message had just come from Johnston. Under orders from President Davis, he had scouted along General Sherman's front. Too strong.

Johnston had decided this was no place for him and pulled out.

Pemberton consulted his division commanders. Were the men fit for an evacuation and a running fight? The replies were unanimous—no. Half the soldiers could not stand.

"Gentlemen," said Pemberton, "I have done what I could." On July 4, 1863, he surrendered.

Paroled under generous terms, John Pemberton would go to Richmond and await a new assignment. Somehow, there never would be a command available in keeping with his rank. He had committed the great sin of his profession: he had failed. So he would do a singular thing, a thing which honor demanded—resign his commission as a lieutenant general. He would serve out the war as a lieutenant colonel, inspecting ordnance.

But that lay in the future. Before reporting to Richmond, he went to see his family in Gainesville, Alabama.

His oldest daughter, Patty, thirteen, was at play in the garden. She stopped bouncing her red and yellow ball to look inquiringly at the man walking up the path.

Who was this stranger with the gray hair?

John Pemberton halted. He remembered. His hair had been black when she had seen him last, five months ago.

After an awful stillness, he held out his hand.

JOHN CLIFFORD PEMBERTON

BORN: Philadelphia, Pennsylvania, August 10, 1814.
DIED: Penllyn, Pennsylvania, July 13, 1881.

THE ILLUSTRATION, PAGE 121: *"Whistling Dick," the pet of the Confederate gunners in the Vicksburg batteries.*

124

Thomas Acton
Police Board President, New York City

29

THE DRAFT RIOTS

BLINDFOLDED by a handkerchief, the chief clerk of the 9th District of New York City, thrust his hand into a revolving drum. From hundreds of slips of paper stuffed inside he pulled out one.

It bore the name, William Jones, and the address, 46th Street and Tenth Avenue. The crowd hooted and flung earthy jibes. William Jones had the unwanted honor of being the first man ever conscripted into the United States Army.

On this Saturday morning, July 11, 1863, New York City was carrying out its obligations under the draft law of March 3. (The year before the Confederacy had resorted to the same measure when not enough volunteers enlisted.) Opponents of the draft had freely predicted violence. But there was no trouble here in the Provost Marshal's office. A few jeers, a few hisses, and some rough humor were all.

The blindfolded clerk went on drawing names. At noon the office closed for

125

the week end. The onlookers drifted out into the hot streets, many to gather in the beer parlor next door. The draft officials grinned smugly. Where was the violence?

The next morning the blindfolded clerk became a shocking reality. The newspapers printed the names of the drafted men. Most were poor Irish immigrants. All day Sunday men grumbled and cursed in cheap saloons on the lower East Side. Mobs began to collect.

Up in his Fifth Avenue mansion, Mayor George Opdyke heard a police sergeant's report. In the Fifth Ward a dozen Negroes had been beaten and several shanties burned.

"Fires are common, and colored people, unfortunately, are often attacked." The Mayor puffed his dollar cigar.

Down on Allen Street a rangy man with a red beard and fine linen clothes spoke to men in dirty shirts. His voice had a Virginia accent. Six fellow conspirators watched craftily as John Andrews, Confederate agent, fanned discontent.

Down with the draft! A brick was thrown and the wildfire of hate shot in all directions. A dark swarm of humanity spilled out of the slums.

Rioters burned the draft building and beat Police Superintendent Kennedy senseless. They poured over the streets armed with crowbars, baling hooks, and clubs. By noon Monday mobs had almost taken over the city.

Thomas Acton stared from the window of the Metropolitan Police Headquarters off Bleecker Street in the downtown area. With Kennedy disabled, Acton held the reins of the city's defense.

An attorney who never practiced, Acton had turned to politics for a livelihood. He had recently risen to president of the police board through the usual appointments: assistant county clerk, deputy register, and police commissioner.

Fortunately, Acton had stamina and the ability to make quick, sure decisions. As he saw smoke rising over his city, he swore softly. Confound if he'd give in to brute force! He turned from the window and snapped his orders.

He had eight hundred policemen to cope with a mob estimated at fifty thousand. His strategy, therefore, was to hoard his men at headquarters and in the lower part of the city to protect the banks. Flying squads would be sent uptown only in extreme emergencies.

He wired the Brooklyn Navy Yard, all military stations within two states, and the Secretary of War. He begged for more troops. The handful of soldiers in the city had to protect Federal depots like the Elm Steet arsenal.

Meanwhile howling mobs ruled the streets, breaking into liquor stores and bars, heading drunkenly for the Matson gun factory. With whisky and guns, they could hold the city.

The rioting flared from a provision in the draft law. It allowed a man to buy his way out for three hundred dollars. Longshoremen and laborers could not hope to raise enough to keep out of the army. The slogan, "It's a rich man's war but a poor man's fight!" went with the mobs. Stores and the homes of the rich became justified targets for looters.

৶৯

Acton's courageous police fought pitched battles all over the city. Their locust sticks split heads and routed gigantic mobs at the Matson gun factory and on Broadway.

But mobs spawned mobs. Drunkenness spurred greed and hate. In the orgy of looting, the original cause was forgotten. Toughs ranted against the Negro. The Negro competed for jobs. The Negro wasn't going to be drafted. Die in some Southern swamp to free the Negro? *Kill* the Negro!

The mob snarled. Any Negro caught alone—man, woman, or child—might be stoned, hanged, roasted, or drowned.

A wire went out to all precincts: "Receive every colored person. Refuse no one—Acton."

Hour after hour he pored over his maps, shifting his police to the danger spots. His men performed unbelievable feats against armed gangs forty times their number. Meanwhile, the Governor, the Board of Aldermen, and the City Council bowed in fright.

The Governor of New York, Horatio Seymour, pathetically promised to have the draft called off. The trembling legislators voted to pay the three hundred dollars of every man drafted. Mayor Opdyke scornfully vetoed the bill.

By Wednesday, traffic moving out of Manhattan had swelled to a stampede. Dazed New Yorkers packed the ferries to Brooklyn and New Jersey. Heavily loaded carriages of wealthy refugees clogged the roads to Westchester.

That night relief arrived. The 74th New York Regiment came in from the battlefield at Gettysburg. A half hour later the 65th Regiment, New York State Militia, followed.

Acton laid out a line of march through the riot-stricken areas. The soldiers, who had grumbled about being on a fool's errand, stared grimly. They saw smoldering huts, barricades, gutted buildings, and bodies. Uptown, stony-faced whites stood in unwelcoming silence. The troops by then tramped in anger. More local units disembarked the next day.

The show of strength and an appeal by Roman Catholic Archbishop John Hughes ended the riot on Friday afternoon. Ironically, the draft was to take only twenty-three hundred New Yorkers. Scarcely more than this number had been injured and killed in the street fighting.

All over the city iron shutters parted on shop windows. Ferries cautiously edged from New Jersey and Brooklyn. The staff of the colored children's orphanage on Forty-third Street shuffled through the wreckage of their building. They talked about constructing a new and bigger home.

Thomas Acton did not see his city beginning to heal. He had fallen fast asleep over his maps.

THOMAS ACTON

Born: New York City, New York, February 23, 1823.
Died: Old Saybrook, Connecticut, May 1, 1898.

The Illustration, Page 125: *A draft riot in New York City.*

John Wilkinson
Lieutenant Commander, Confederate States of America

30

BLOCKADE RUNNER

JOHN WILKINSON padded into the darkened wheelhouse. He squinted through a peephole in the canvas that blocked light off the compass. Satisfied, he nodded at his helmsman and returned to the bridge.

Talk aboard the *Robert E. Lee* sounded in hushed tones. To reduce deck noise, Wilkinson had donned slippers. Every other precaution had been taken to insure secrecy, down to muffling the ship's clock and masking all lights. Tarpaulins covered ventilators, companionways, and hatches. Below deck, the crew sweated in hot, foul air.

Wilkinson, a burly, mustachioed, Latin-quoting Virginian, gazed up into the night sky. Once at sea, he took his own celestial sightings and time readings. He plotted his course from charts he had helped bring up to date as a United States Navy officer before the war. A master sailor, he trusted no one. By doing the vital jobs himself, he had achieved phenomenal success in eluding the Union blockading fleets.

This night, August 15, 1863, he had sailed from Wilmington, North Carolina. The wharves there bulked high with thousands of bales of cotton, tierces of tobacco, and barrels of turpentine—the prime offerings of the Confederacy.

Via the fog-colored hulls of the blockade runners, Southern goods were sold at the neutral warehouse ports of Bermuda, Nassau, and Halifax. Cargoes on the return trip were the materials of war.

Wilkinson had cotton in his hold. Deftly he skirted the blockaders off the New Inlet Bar. In the darkness of the moon, the shots fired by the Yankees dropped wide.

At dawn, thirty miles out from the coast, Wilkinson heard news he did not like. The last of the good English coal had been consumed. The ship had to switch to smoky, fast-burning North Carolina coal.

The change-over had just been completed when the lookout sang, "Sail ho!" Wilkinson cried back, "Where away?" and from the masthead came, "Right astern, sir, and in chase."

Wilkinson scrambled to the crow's-nest. He descried a cruiser, which he learned later was the U.S.S. *Iroquois*. Her topgallant grew above the horizon.

"She'll be alongside us by midday," Wilkinson muttered, and spat a line from Virgil. He ordered the deckside cotton thrown overboard to lighten the load, and more steam made. The first was easily done; the second was impossible, owing to the wretched coal.

The *Robert E. Lee* ranked among the finest and fastest blockade runners. Wilkinson had chosen her himself and bought her for the Confederacy in Glasgow, Scotland. With her double stacks, paddle wheels, and two-masted sail, she ought to have outrun the big square-rigger giving chase.

Her top speed was thirteen and a half knots. Burning North Carolina coal, she generated no better than eight knots. If only there were another fuel. . . .

Wilkinson's eyes rested upon the cotton. Why not? "Let's try it, saturated with spirits of turpentine," he suggested to his chief engineer.

A bale was opened, soaked, and passed to the engine room by bucket brigade. The intense heat produced a full pressure of steam. Thirteen and a half knots was reached within five minutes. The cruiser ceased to gain.

By six o'clock the position of the two ships had altered little. Suddenly the *Lee* slowed. The burned cotton had choked the flues. The pressure dropped swiftly, and she lay almost unmoving. The cruiser drew near.

"Keep her going till dark," Wilkinson ordered the chief engineer.

He limped across the bridge. The overheated boilers had fired the deck. His feet in the thin slippers were about to blister. But off to the southeast he had seen hope.

A dark cloud floated at the horizon. Another hour and it would be twilight. He could slip pursuit in those clouds.

"Give me as much smoke as you can," he told the engine room. The response was a great billowing that hid the ship. As twilight deepened into night, two officers he had posted by the wheelhouse shouted in unison: "We've lost sight of her!"

Instantly Wilkinson cried, "Close the dampers!" The smoke was cut off. Wilkinson swung his ship at right angles to the old course, leaving the cruiser to chase a boatless trail of smoke into the night.

ঙ৽

ALTHOUGH he had foxed the Yankees again, Wilkinson did not underestimate his foe. The *Iroquois* would try to catch him off Abaco Light on the way to Nassau. So he veered for Bermuda.

Two days later he entered St. George Harbor and dropped anchor.

Blockade runners of every description rode quietly in the water. They were manned by crews of "high wages and low character." Fabulous overnight profits were the lure. A quarter million dollars could be realized on each leg of the seven-day round trip.

After directing the unloading barges alongside the *Lee*, Wilkinson rowed wearily ashore. He stopped first at the warehouse of John Tory Bourne, the local agent for the Confederate government.

Smiling, Wilkinson read the labels on the crates. *Merchandise* was European rifles, *combustibles* were gunpowder, and *nails* were lead for bullets. The warehouse was stacked to the rafters with crates falsely marked.

Wilkinson reported his cargo. Then he took the path that led to a little whitewashed hotel and a good night's sleep. Within two days he would be sailing for Wilmington. The homeward trip was the risky one. Inbound cargoes usually included gunpowder. A lucky shot might sink investments and adventurers early. And the Union blockade was steadily strengthening.

The blockade had been created to strangle Southern commerce. In 1861 the Union had only forty-two vessels to patrol thirty-six hundred miles of coast, a hundred and eighty-nine rivers, and innumerable bays and inlets. Nine out of ten runners got to Southern ports. By the war's end, sixteen hundred new Union ships would join the blockading squadrons. Still, two out of three runners would make it to port.

All in all, six hundred thousand stands of small arms, plus all the requirements of a war machine, would be landed by the Confederacy. In four years of blockade running, sixteen hundred and fifty ships would make eight thousand successful round trips.

Some sort of record belongs to John Wilkinson. He ran twenty-one round trips in ten months. The tricks by which he baffled his pursuers were widely copied by other skippers throughout the war on the seas.

❧❧❧ • ❧❧❧

JOHN WILKINSON

BORN: Norfolk, Virginia, November 6, 1821.
DIED: Annapolis, Maryland, December 29, 1891.

THE ILLUSTRATION, PAGE 129: *Wilkinson's ship "Robert E. Lee" with a map of the blockade of Atlantic coast of the Confederacy.*

Christopher Miner Spencer
Inventor

31
WONDER GUN

IN THE FALL of 1862 a deadly new sound entered the war.

The first soldiers to hear it were the men of the 1st Massachusetts Cavalry. Near Cumberland, Maryland, Sergeant Francis O. Lombard shot what looked like a slimmed-down musket. Only it loaded from the wrong end. And when the sergeant squeezed the trigger, he sounded like a whole squad.

Two thousand of the sensational guns showed up later in a full-scale battle near Chattanooga, Tennessee. John Thomas Wilder's "Lightning Brigade"

repulsed five times as many Confederates. The solid Gray lines rushed forward in the customary closed ranks, and shattered. Although no one realized it that day, the infantry charge had become obsolete under the terrible fire power of Wilder's men.

The oddest part of both episodes is that the revolutionary gun—a repeating rifle—was not an official weapon of the United States Army!

Wilder had ordered the guns privately, paying thirty-five dollars apiece for them out of his own pocket. Ser-

133

geant Lombard, a former gunsmith, had been given the gun to try out by his friend, Christopher Spencer.

A quiet little Connecticut Yankee, Spencer invented things as naturally as he breathed. About the time Sergeant Lombard was sighting his repeater, Spencer was making news of a different kind. He was causing the nation's first automobile accident.

Spencer had developed a steam-driven auto. A rude differential allowed him to zoom around corners at full speed. With a wide grin on his face and a heavy hand on the steering tiller, he terrorized the pedestrians of Boston. Then the grandfather of all hot rods smashed into a milk wagon and ended Spencer's quest for speed.

The quest for the perfect firearm had occupied him since boyhood. Since 1849 he had learned to handle tools and machinery by working in Charles Cheney's silk mills in Manchester, Connecticut, and in the Colt Firearms Company in Hartford. In March, 1860, he had received patent No. 27,393 for a repeating, or self-loading, rifle.

He had a patent and a rifle of overwhelming potential. But he could not interest the logical customer, the United States Army.

"A newfangled gimcrack," pronounced aged Brigadier General James W. Ripley, chief of the Bureau of Ordnance. Ripley was a veteran of four wars and fifty years of Army service. He championed the ancient smoothbore muzzle-loaders with the stubbornness of a man arguing for sail over steam.

Helped by his old employer, Charles Cheney, Spencer got his first big break in June, 1861. He demonstrated his repeater at the Washington Navy Yard.

Navy officials watched in awe as he twice fired two hundred and fifty rounds without stopping to swab the barrel. The result: an order for seven hundred repeaters.

With Cheney's backing, Spencer rented half the Chickering piano plant in Boston and installed an assembly line. Before the war ended, he had turned out ten thousand of his guns for the Navy. Yet he still had not sold the Army, where, he felt, the repeater could do the most good in shortening the war.

❧

IT WAS NOW 1862. Sergeant Lombard proved the gun in Maryland. Wilder's men ripped the Confederates in Tennessee. In Washington, old General Ripley went on purchasing firearms with the foresight of a dinosaur.

Charles Cheney again used his influence. Working outside Ripley's reach, he arranged for a cross-service deal. The Navy shipped the Army several thousand repeaters. Five thousand arrived in time to play a vital part during the first and third days at Gettysburg.

Ripley still wasn't interested. Spencer faced bankruptcy or the shutdown of his Boston factory. Cheney wangled an interview with the President himself.

On the morning of August 17, 1863, Spencer was ushered into the President's office.

"He appeared to be expecting me," said the gunsmith. "Without a moment's delay he took the gun out of my hands. When he asked me to 'show the inwardness of the thing,' he was greatly impressed that all I needed was a screw driver."

Lincoln invited Spencer to return the next day at 2:00 P.M., when, he said, "We will go out and see the thing shoot." The next day, on an improvised range near the Washington Monument, the Chief Executive watched shooting, repeater style.

The basic weapon of both armies till then was the single-shot, .58-caliber, muzzle-loading rifle. Bullet and powder were wrapped in paper for easy loading. A percussion cap set off the charge.

Three rounds a minute was considered fast shooting.

Spencer's seven-shot, lever-action gun fired from five to seven times as fast, and was shorter and lighter. Seven .52-caliber cartridges were held in a tubular magazine which fed into the breech through the wood butt. Outfitted with a box of ten spare magazines, a soldier could shoot seventy rounds at rapid fire.

The Presidential target was a smooth pine board three feet long and six inches high. A black smudge at one end marked the bull's-eye.

From forty yards Lincoln's first shot hit left and five inches low. His second pierced the bull's-eye, and the other five clustered around it.

After the test, he marched triumphantly into the White House, the gun over his shoulder. Within a month, old General Ripley was "retired."

Orders from the Army poured in upon Christopher Spencer. More than seventy-five thousand of his repeaters got into the war. There were other rapid-fire guns, but they appeared too late to affect the outcome. Among these were Tyler Henry's and the so-called "machine gun" of Richard Gatling.

By 1864, the Spencer carbine was the standard arm of the Union cavalry. It was easy to load on horseback. It gave the Blue horsemen, who were fighting better all the time, just the edge necessary to dominate the Gray.

It did not matter that some of the wonder guns fell into Confederate hands. Captured Spencers were useless to the Southerners. The metal Spencer cartridge was the first completely self-contained cartridge, and the South lacked the means to manufacture it.

"The Spencer carbines fully doubled the efficiency of the cavalry against ours," bemoaned one Confederate general.

And with the wistful humor that so often had to make up for shortages of food, clothing, and weapons, one Johnny Reb declared:

"Those confounded Yankees loaded up their guns in the morning and shot all day."

CHRISTOPHER MINER SPENCER

> BORN: Manchester, Connecticut, June 20, 1833.
> DIED: Hartford, Connecticut, January 14, 1922.

THE ILLUSTRATION, PAGE 133: *The Spencer rifle showing bullets and firing pin.*

Kate Chase
Society Belle

32

BELLE OF WASHINGTON

FATE SMILED in the beginning. It endowed Kate Chase with wit and beauty. Her father, Lincoln's Secretary of the Treasury, added position and influence. Kate herself supplied the most important part of all—ambition.

With all her forces dedicated to helping her father become President, Kate reigned over Washington society throughout the years of the war.

By the summer of 1863, Kate was the most envied young lady in the capital. After breaking countless hearts, "the prettiest Kate in Christendom" had finally been wooed and won. The young man was wealthy William Sprague, III, lately Boy Governor of Rhode Island and now United States Senator. Shopgirls hastened through the news from the battlefields to read about the romance.

As the wedding day approached, Kate gave no thought to limiting her activities. If anything, she visited the camps around the city more frequently. She enriched the drab existence there by lunching with all the right generals.

Sparkling though she was with the

137

military, it was in parlors befogged with cigar smoke that Kate really blazed. Behind the lovely face was a mind as hard and able as any in Washington.

As her widowed father's hostess, Kate officially ranked fourth on Washington's social ladder. Yet she skipped blithely to the top. Brilliance, charm, and beauty lifted her past everyone, including Mrs. Lincoln.

The First Lady had smarted since Kate's arrival in Washington in 1861. She had bitten her lip often as Kate held court at the White House receptions. Before long the gayest parties were not the ones at the White House, but at the mansion of the Secretary of the Treasury.

The Chases, father and daughter, hunted the Presidency and made little secret of it. The New York *Herald* observed that Mrs. Lincoln should good-naturedly allow Kate to hold her wedding reception in the East Room of the White House. This kindness, said the *Herald*, would give Kate "an opportunity of judging how it suits her."

Kate's wedding to Sprague was pronounced the most brilliant social function of the war. Secretary of the Navy Gideon Welles was one of those who viewed the affair with an undazzled eye. He commented dryly: "Few young men have such advantages as he, and Miss Kate has talents and ambitions sufficient for both."

The ceremony was scheduled to start at 8:30 P.M. For an hour before that time the long line of carriages crept up to the Chase door. Cabinet members, generals, and diplomats, along with their bejeweled and silk-clad ladies, descended the carriage steps, trod radiantly across the matting that led to the door, and disappeared into the mansion.

The President arrived late, unaccompanied by Mrs. Lincoln. Seconds after he entered, the wedding began. The crowd on the street thrilled to the "Kate Chase Wedding March," written especially for the bride.

Kate was never lovelier. Her large hazel eyes and magnificent lashes, her auburn hair pulled back in a bun, her tilted nose and slender, proud figure— all were set off by an exquisite gown which featured a long velvet train. Her lace veil was held by a clasp of pearls and diamonds, a present from the groom.

As for Sprague, those seeing him for the first time experienced some disappointment. Small, stooped, and nearsighted, he little resembled the stalwart young warrior-statesman of newspaper accounts. His face had a vague weakness. In one less wealthy, the look might have been blamed on whisky.

In truth, young Senator Sprague owed his high standing to virtues other than ability. He had inherited twenty-five million dollars and several cotton mills. To this inheritance, it was whispered, he also owed his bride.

The whispers were accurate enough. Suave Salmon P. Chase did not mean to be beaten out of the Presidency in 1864 as he had been in 1860, by an awkward backwoods lawyer. Many Republicans, discontented with Lincoln, looked to Chase for leadership. But leadership required money. Kate's wedding cost four thousand dollars. Salmon Chase was in debt, and his son-in-law had twenty-five millions.

Lincoln was warned repeatedly about his Secretary of the Treasury. He refused to oust him. "Mr. Chase makes a good Secretary," the President said, "and I shall keep him where he is. If he becomes President, all right, I hope we may never have a worse man."

Chase was not to win the nomination in 1864. His supporters erred. They attacked Lincoln so harshly that the President's popularity, instead of declining, soared.

Chase submitted his resignation, which was promptly accepted. Lincoln then appointed him Chief Justice of the Supreme Court to keep him from plotting further mischief.

WHEN THE NEWS of the appointment was brought to the Chase home, Kate was dining there. Pale and thin, she had just recovered from an illness brought on by the defeat in the Presidential campaign. She shook her finger at Senator Charles Sumner, who had delivered the tidings of her father's new office.

"And you, too, Mr. Sumner?" she scolded. "You, too, in this business of shelving Papa? But never mind. I will defeat you all!"

Largely because of Kate, Chase attempted to win the 1868 nomination. He failed, though many believed he would have won had Kate been allowed on the convention floor. His electioneering while on the high court bench damaged his reputation beyond repair. He died in 1873.

That same year the panic wiped out nearly all of William Sprague's fortune. His marriage to Kate had collapsed several years earlier. Treasonable wartime dealings, heavy drinking, and his inability to outrank Salmon Chase in

Kate's affections resulted in a divorce in 1882. Sprague died in Paris in 1915, ruined in both mind and body.

Kate lived out her life in Edgewood, her father's home in Washington. The dignitaries whom she had charmed in the glittering days of her beauty were long dead. The war itself was a tired subject of conversation. The people of Washington, if they noticed her at all, saw only a tall woman in a plumed hat.

Her kid gloves hid work-coarsened hands.

From the heights, Kate Chase plunged to the depths.

In 1896 Henry Villard, a family friend, raised money to pay her mortgage at Edgewood. Thereafter Kate had some security with which to enjoy her memories. For the three years left her, she eked out an existence selling eggs and milk.

KATE CHASE

BORN: Cincinnati, Ohio, August 13, 1840.
DIED: Washington, D.C., July 31, 1899.

THE ILLUSTRATION, PAGE 137: *Kate Chase visiting General John J. Abercrombie's headquarters.*

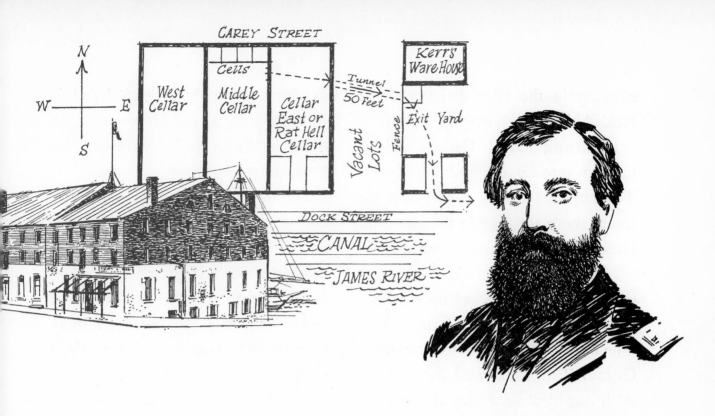

Thomas Ellwood Rose
Colonel, United States of America

33

TUNNEL UNDER LIBBY

ALTHOUGH it was February, and an icy wind beat against Libby Prison, Colonel Tom Rose's face glistened with perspiration. Deep within the shoulder-wide tunnel the air was hot and poisonous.

He tugged on the clotheslines. After a moment came the response to his signal. The wood spittoon with its freight of sandy earth was hauled out.

Rose pocketed his "shovel," a chipped and rusty chisel. He pushed his palms into the gritty tunnel floor and wormed backward. Helping hands caught his ankles and pulled him the last body length.

Straightening onto his feet, he drew breath in the huge black cellar of the prison. His lungs filled with air that was clean only compared to the stench in the tunnel. He flexed and stretched his limbs.

"I make it another three days," he announced quietly.

Hope of escape sped like an electric flash through the four Union officers

141

standing in the inky darkness. Each tackled his job with new enthusiasm.

Lieutenant David Garbett, whose turn it was to dig, dropped to his knees. The entrance of the tunnel was six inches above the floor in the east wall. Grunting, he squirmed forward.

Major A. G. Hamilton, Rose's second in command, picked up a rubber blanket stretched over a frame. With it he began fanning air into the tunnel. Captain B. B. McDonald dumped the earth dug by Rose, hiding it under the straw that carpeted the floor to a depth of two feet. He put the empty spittoon in Garbett's hand.

At the opposite wall, Rose was already ascending a rope ladder to the floor above. He emerged through a fireplace converted into a hatchway by the removal of a dozen bricks. When the sentries outside called four o'clock, Major Hamilton and his team would climb up the same way, replacing the bricks behind them.

Noiselessly, Rose mounted two flights of stairs. As he got to his loft, one of nine in the former warehouse, he heard a familiar order.

"Attention, squad three! Prepare to spoon! One, two, three—spoon!"

There were muffled thuds as the closely lying men flopped over, changing from their right sides to their left. Rose furtively picked his way over the crowded forms and lay down, exhausted.

He felt as if he had only closed his eyes when Captain Isaac Johnson woke him.

"There was a bigger party of Confederates than usual in the cellar last night," Johnston whispered. "I think they suspect something. One of them walked right by the hole. Luckily he didn't see it in the darkness."

Rose immediately warned all the members of the escape party to remain upstairs. He and McDonald returned at once to the rat-infested cellar.

Rose inched himself into the tunnel, and from that moment forward he did not ask relief. McDonald, his lone helper, performed double duty. He fanned air into the tunnel and hid the excavated dirt.

Whereas the threat of discovery overburdened McDonald and the others, it spurred Rose to superhuman effort. A mild man ordinarily, he sometimes roused himself with astonishing results. What he was about to do eclipsed anything he had done before.

The eastern tunnel was actually his fourth attempt at escape. Sentries, water, and heavy timbers had thwarted him before. In the three months of his imprisonment, he had grimly withstood every setback. He had outwitted the guards. And what was infinitely more difficult, he had kept secret his efforts from the mass of his fellow inmates. Twelve hundred prisoners clamoring for freedom could upset everything.

Now, after boring into the earth for two weeks, the unbeatable Pennsylvanian sensed that success was near. He jabbed and twisted the chisel, burrowing like a mole. His mind filled with the pressure of one pounding instinct— freedom.

McDonald was weak with fatigue and giddy from the noisome cellar when Tom Rose finally backed out. He staggered to his feet. "We better take a night's rest," he mumbled.

Upstairs, the thirteen other plotters heard the day's news with quickening hope. Rose, toiling alone, had dug twice as far as had ever been dug in a day by the system of three shifts. And the Confederates had not appeared.

❧

AT DAWN Rose and McDonald were back in the cellar. Then began an epic of stamina and determination that has few rivals. From early morning on February 8, 1864, until one o'clock the next morning, Tom Rose lay on his stomach in total darkness and hacked at the reeking earth ahead of him.

After twenty-four hours every muscle quivered with pain and exhaustion. Every breath sickened him. The faint current of air from McDonald's fan could not reach him through fifty feet of tunnel.

When Rose estimated he had dug far enough, he altered to an upward course. To give his tortured limbs relief, he rolled on his back. All at once he felt himself blacking out.

The chisel slipped from his fingers. The strength to back out had drained from him. Trapped, suffocating, he smashed both fists against the tunnel roof in an agonized burst of strength.

The crust of earth above him broke and showered on his discolored face. Cool air poured over him. He saw a star!

Panting like a drowning man, Rose heaved himself out of the hole. He had come up exactly where he had planned: in a yard between the office of the James River Towing Company and a shed of Kerr's warehouse. Behind him a fence walled off Libby Prison and the guards.

The open road to freedom beckoned. But Tom Rose, who had risen from private to colonel of the 77th Pennsylvania Volunteers, did not desert McDonald and the others. After a hasty reconnoiter, he slipped back into the tunnel, drawing a plank over the hole after him.

The rest of the party heard his tiding with tears of joy. At seven o'clock that evening, they followed Rose into the tunnel and out upon the streets of Richmond. So did nearly a hundred others who had got the "tip" that day.

Of the 109 who squirmed to liberty, 48 reached Union lines. It would be nice to say that Colonel Thomas Rose was among the successful.

Limping upon a painfully swollen foot, he was recaptured near Williamsburg, Virginia, a mile from Union pickets. Returned to Libby Prison, he was locked in a solitary cell.

THOMAS ELLWOOD ROSE

BORN: Haverford, Pennsylvania, 1830 (?).
DIED: Washington, D.C., November, 1907.

THE ILLUSTRATION, PAGE 141: *Libby Prison as it appeared at the time of Rose's escape, with ground plan showing escape route.*

The *H. L. Hunley*

34

SUBMARINE FROM THE SOUTH

A SMALL GROUP of Southerners stood on the bank of the Mobile River. Their eyes were trained on an old flatboat anchored in midstream. As the men watched, the flatboat suddenly burst apart. Pieces flew a hundred feet in the air.

A little while later a weird shape broke surface downstream. A hatch opened, and a man's head and shoulders emerged into the fresh air. He waved triumphantly. The men on shore waved back. Then they shook hands all around.

The submarine *H. L. Hunley* had passed the test. At last the South had a deadly undersea answer to the Union fleets blockading its coasts and waterways.

All was not quite perfect, however. The first trial had been conducted in the calm Mobile River. When taken out in the rough bay, the little *Hunley* exhibited an unhealthy quirk. She was constantly on the verge of swamping. Mobile, obviously, was not a promising field of operations.

Her sponsors decided to take her overland to Charleston. No port in the South had greater need of assistance. The North had the harbor plugged with a double line of ironclads and wooden ships. Here was the ideal spot to spread terror in the Union Navy, and to make a fortune besides.

For there was money in the invention —if it worked. President Jefferson Davis had urged citizens to take up the fight against enemy ships. His government guaranteed to pay handsomely for every Union man-of-war sunk.

Out of the twin motives of profit and patriotism had come the *Hunley*. Her builders, James R. McClintock and Baxter Watson of New Orleans, had run out of funds before the boat was completed. They'd had to appeal to outsiders. The biggest investor was Horace L. Hunley, and for him the submarine was named.

From Mobile the *Hunley* was transported on two railroad flatcars, and she arrived at Charleston in the summer of 1863. General P. G. T. Beauregard, commanding the city's defenses, agreed to give the privately owned boat a crack at the Union fleet.

A crew was enlisted under John Payne, an army lieutenant, and the first practice run began. As Payne prepared to close the forward hatch, a steamer passed close by. Her swell flooded over the deck of the low-riding *Hunley*. Payne scampered to safety as water poured into the open hatch. While he swam to the wharf, the submarine sank with her crew.

Payne got permission to try again. The *Hunley* was retrieved from the deep and repaired. With a new crew she started off on a shakedown run. Again she sank. Payne and two of the crew escaped.

By now fourteen men had died in the submarine. Beauregard wished to leave the sea-going coffin at the bottom of the harbor. But from Mobile came Horace Hunley. He brought along a crew experienced in handling his namesake. He insisted the boat was sound. On October 15, before a large crowd, he got the machine into the water, dived—and never came up.

This time General Beauregard ordered the experiments stopped. But two engineers, Dixon and Alexander, begged for one more chance. They had helped build the submarine at Mobile, and they believed they could find the trouble.

The pair examined the *Hunley* carefully and became convinced they knew how to make the coffin surface. Under their direction the boat was overhauled.

A new crew was raised, though Beauregard demanded that the past tragedies of the *Hunley* be fully recounted to every potential volunteer.

⌇

IN THE FOLLOWING weeks, it seemed the *Hunley* had broken her habit of sinking. She ventured out six and seven miles. Always she was forced to turn back without using her torpedo, however. Rough seas threatened to sweep her away from land before she reached a Union ship.

November and December dragged by. Dixon and Alexander doggedly waited for ideal conditions—a dark and calm night. They planned to ride out on the ebb tide, release the torpedo, and ride in on the flood tide. The weather remained against them. Toward the close of January, 1864, Alexander was forced to return to Mobile. Dixon stayed on with growing impatience.

On the night of February 17, the wind died down and the sea calmed. Despite a full moon, which might reveal the submarine in the water, Dixon elected to go out.

The crew entered by the fore and aft hatches and took their places at the ship-long propeller shaft, facing the rear. They laid their hands on the levers set in the shaft and waited for the order to begin cranking the propeller.

Dixon dropped aboard by the forward hatch, the second officer by the rear one. They made the craft tight and let water into the ballast tanks. The boat settled to three inches below water level. Then the second officer took his seat and the cranking started.

Meantime, Dixon in the front had lighted a candle to provide illumination and to show any failure in the oxygen supply, which was good for at least two and a half hours. Next he turned the lever which operated the fins, and the *Hunley* submerged.

Driven by muscle power, the boat slid through the water at top speed, four knots. Dixon watched the mercury gauge which showed the depth. Now and again he peered through the skylight in the hatch above him.

Shortly before nine o'clock, Acting Master J. K. Crosby was standing on the deck of the Union sloop-of-war *Housatonic*. His attention was attracted by a ruffle on the moonlit water about a hundred yards away. At first he thought it a large fish or plank. When the thing came straight on, he sounded the alarm. Word of the *Hunley* had been leaked by a Confederate deserter, and Crosby wanted to be on the safe side.

The beat to quarters brought Captain Charles W. Pickering on deck. Crosby pointed out the mysterious shape in the water. Pickering ordered the engines started. The ship's guns were directed on the approaching menace, but the *Hunley* was so close the guns could not be lowered enough to score a hit. Men fired with rifles and revolvers.

As the *Housatonic* desperately backed away, the *Hunley*, for some unknown reason, changed course. As a result, sloop and submarine came together.

The blast knocked the men of the *Housatonic* flat. The whole ship seemed to blow apart. She sank almost at once, black smoke billowing from her stack. Amazingly, all save five of her crew were rescued.

What had happened to the *Hunley?* No trace of her was found for years. Then she was discovered on the bottom, lying with her prow toward the wreck of the *Housatonic*. She had perished in the explosion, drowning the last of her dauntless crews.

The death of the *Housatonic* marked a new page in naval warfare. Never before had an underwater craft sunk a warship. Not for fifty years would another submarine repeat the feat.

THE ILLUSTRATION, PAGE 145: *The submarine torpedo boat, "H. L. Hunley."*

Montgomery Cunningham Meigs
Major General, United States of America

35

FIVE HUNDRED HORSES A DAY

THE MARE had a coarse head, small sunken eyes, and a hollow back.

"Ringbone," said Montgomery Meigs, running his long fingers over her fetlock and coronet. "And judging by the purplish hue of her nostrils, Mr. Conners, she's got pneumonia. You paid one hundred and ten dollars of government money for an animal that might not live another week."

"You have to take what you can get these days, General," John Conners re-

torted sulkily. He hadn't expected Meigs to stop by. Another half hour and he would have had the horses on the way to the field.

Meigs jotted in his notebook. Then he strode from the corral.

Of the hundred horses ready to be shipped, forty-eight were sound. Meigs judged the others unfit. His notebook contained such comments as *too young, too old, too thin, spavined,* and *thoroughly used up.*

When he returned to his office, he

149

scribbled a message to Major D. H. Rucker, head of the Washington quartermaster depot.

Discharge Conners and all civilian inspectors of horses at once.

Meigs had long suspected what he could not prove: the inspectors were taking bribes for passing animals of poor quality. After enough complaints, he had seen for himself.

His surprise visit to the corral was but a small part of his job. On the whole that job was, after the Presidency, the most difficult in the Union.

As quartermaster general he had to clothe, feed, and transport an army that in the first four months of the war grew twenty-eight times—from 17,113 men to 485,650!

And he had to stamp out the bloodsucker of corruption.

Only a man with Meigs's absolute devotion to duty could have succeeded in the double task. The Union forces never met defeat for want of supplies. And once the fantastic growth of the army ceased, profiteering was held in check.

In the beginning dishonesty had legal help. The law allowed contracts to be given without competitive bidding. Furthermore, generals cared little how materials were obtained so long as enough was on hand when needed. Lumber, coal, clothing, and horses were bought at one price and billed to the government at a higher price. The agent pocketed the difference or split with the contractor. Contracts were given to favored suppliers as a matter of course.

To curb such evils, Meigs recommended the following:

"If forage, wagons, or horses are wanted, the law and necessity are fully met by putting a notice in the paper and purchasing as fast as offers come in. The next day or the same day take the then lowest bidder or the most advantageous offer. The next day you will have a still better offer. Take that for a portion of your supplies, and so on until you have all you need. By this system I have brought down the prices of horses from $128 to $120, of wagons from $141 to $108 . . . and have got abundant supplies."

Meigs's stanch honesty may be traced to his parents, respected Philadelphians of Puritan stock. They reared him in the strict traditions of loyalty to country and regard for duty. At West Point he graduated fifth in his class and acquired an engineer's exactness of mind.

As a civilian engineer, he might have commanded a large salary. He preferred to stay in the army. From 1852 on he worked on projects in Washington. He was chief engineer in the early construction of the Washington Aqueduct, which supplied Washington with water. He also supervised the building of the wings and dome of the Capitol and the enlargement of the Post Office building.

His work showed him to be a man of ability and principle, virtues which on occasion cause some politicians to shy off. To his credit as a diplomat, he won political backing and respect. When Joseph E. Johnston resigned as quartermaster general to join the Confederacy, Meigs was appointed his successor.

Brigadier General Meigs walked into a department of thirteen clerks. They were accustomed to handling four to five million dollars a year. By the end of the war, Meigs had an overworked staff of 591. Spending had ballooned to a total of $1,500,000,000.

❧

MEIGS took over a department not only understaffed but underranked and organized as aimlessly as "a flock of sheep." Junior officers in the department frequently had more responsibility than brigadier generals of infantry. For several weeks the depot quartermaster at Washington had nine thousand men under him—yet his rank was only captain!

Every brigade, division, and corps in the field had its own supply depot and quartermaster officer. The officers purchased what was needed and sent monthly statements to Meigs in Washington. Hence 3,600 statements a year had to be examined and acted upon. The yearly rate of clothing returns amounted to forty thousand.

For three years Meigs made do with the rickety, outdated structure he had inherited. On July 4, 1864, he finally got his reorganization plan approved by Congress, as well as higher rank and pay for his officers. Along the way, he had weeded out corrupt agents (usually civilians; misconduct among Regular Army officers was rare). He had found honest manufacturers and saved the government millions.

Except when Jubal Early briefly threatened Washington in 1864, Meigs never led troops to combat (and then only clerks and invalids). He fought the war from a desk, in a fusillade of papers. His name never appeared in headlines; he wore no medal. In Washington he was taken for granted; in the nation at large he was unknown; in history he has been forgotten.

Without him, the great advantage the North held in resources might have been wasted. He bought and distributed clothing, forage, food, wagons, and fuel. He moved goods on the ocean, rivers, and rails from New York to Texas. He raised hospitals and barracks and conducted endless inspections. In the last year of the war he sent five hundred horses a day to the armies in the field.

Never before was so much money spent on the word of one officer.

"Without the services of this eminent soldier," said Secretary of State William Seward, "the national cause must have been lost or deeply imperiled."

Congress, too, understood the measure of Meigs's devotion.

When a committee got around to investigating the quartermaster department, it could not find one penny unaccounted for.

MONTGOMERY CUNNINGHAM MEIGS

> BORN: Augusta, Georgia, May 3, 1816.
> DIED: Washington, D. C., January 2, 1892.

THE ILLUSTRATION, PAGE 149: *A roundup of horses, purchased for the Union cavalry.*

Ulric Dahlgren
Colonel, United States of America

36

AN END TO KNIGHTHOOD

IN MID-FEBRUARY of 1864 a young officer limped off the train at Brandy Station, Virginia. He ordered a horse, strapped his crutch to the saddle, heaved himself astride, and galloped off in pursuit of fame.

This youth was Ulric Dahlgren, said to be the youngest colonel in the Union Army. He was much favored in high places, for his father was an admiral. Secretary Stanton had personally launched Ulric's war career with a commission as captain.

To his credit, young Dahlgren had proved a nervy soldier. At Boonsboro, Maryland, he had lost his right leg below the knee. While convalescing in Washington, he had been visited by President Lincoln, supplied with a wooden leg, and elevated to colonel.

He had also got wind of a forthcoming "secret" raid into Richmond. A brigadier general of cavalry, Judson Kilpatrick, planned to liberate the 16,500 Union prisoners in the city's two prisons, Belle Isle and Libby Prison.

Many top generals were calling the plan foolhardy. But Abraham Lincoln,

153

deeply concerned about the prisoners, told Kilpatrick to have a try.

There was the chance, given secrecy and rapidity, that the raid might succeed. Lee was wintered too far from Richmond to help defend it against a darting blow. Clerks and bookkeepers would have to man the fortifications around the city.

The stroke would make its leaders the darlings of the nation, or so Ulric Dahlgren believed. Hence he went down to Brandy Station to seek out General Kilpatrick.

Kilpatrick's headquarters in close-by Stevensburg were no trouble to locate. The army lay mud-bound in its winter camps, but the young general passed the days in a spotless mansion.

Kilpatrick had a nickname—Kill Cavalry. He drove men and horses hard. He was a small, politically ambitious man with large ears, thin gingery hair, a loud voice, and a determination to win.

The twenty-eight-year-old general studied the twenty-one-year-old colonel and was pleased. This admiral's son with his fine record and appearance was tailored to order. Ulric Dahlgren would lend the long-shot raid just the public approval it needed.

Everything was arranged. The Union Army began feinting movements to fool the Confederates. At 6:00 P.M. on February 28 Colonel Dahlgren led an advance guard of five hundred picked troopers out from the lines. An hour later General Kilpatrick followed with more than three thousand men, three wagons, four ambulances, eight caissons, and six guns.

Each trooper had three days' rations in his saddlebags and a bright, lofty goal before his eyes. The luster of a medieval quest shimmered along the columns of troopers. They were riding into the enemy's stronghold to rescue their comrades.

The Confederate pickets along the Rapidan River were bagged without a shot sounding. The Blue columns completed the river crossing at Ely's Ford by 1:00 A.M. February 29.

Kilpatrick sent back a message. "It was a complete surprise. No alarm was given. The enemy does not anticipate our movement."

The plan called for Kilpatrick to leave Dahlgren's trail below Spotsylvania and strike Richmond from the north. Dahlgren would press southward, burning and destroying, pivot left at Goochland, and lance in from the west by 10:00 A.M. Tuesday, March 1.

SUNDAY NIGHT bloomed with stars, and the day that followed shone brilliantly. Young Ulric Dahlgren found war to be a grand game. Toward late afternoon, however, the sky darkened. Rain turned to sleet.

Keeping to schedule, Dahlgren reached the James River. Some of his men went ahead, burning canal boats and mills. The others rode among the fine estates of the area setting fires. Dahlgren paused at Sabot Hill, the estate of Confederate Secretary of War James Seddon. Mrs. Seddon was at home. The charming blond colonel, it turned out, was the son of an old beau, Admiral John Dahlgren.

So while his men burned the Seddon barn, Ulric Dahlgren sat in the Seddon drawing room and sipped wine. It was pleasant and warm and dry. But there were prisoners to be rescued. The bold young knight-errant sighed, bowed, and departed.

According to Dahlgren's Negro guide, Martin Robinson, a ford existed in the James River directly on the route to Belle Isle. He showed the blond colonel the place.

He pointed. The river rushed high, swollen by rains . . . Where normally men could cross, Dahlgren saw water ten feet deep.

For the young colonel the knightly role ended there in the cold darkness by the foaming river. It ended in blind fury and the conviction of the guide's treachery. He cut a strap from his bridle.

In a moment the affair was done. The unfortunate Martin Robinson swung by his neck from a tree. The column galloped along the north bank of the James toward Richmond, desperately.

Dahlgren heard artillery. He believed he might yet snatch a cup of glory. But the hour had passed. Kilpatrick, having waited as long as he dared under Richmond's guns, had fallen back. The attempt to release the prisoners wilted, a dismal failure. Dahlgren ordered a withdrawal.

Three hundred got through to Kilpatrick. Dahlgren and the rest rode into an ambush. The blond knight died in a ditch, his feet against a fence rail, five buckshot in his back.

The shots attracted a boy, William Littlepage, thirteen. He crept through the night in search of souvenirs. On a dead Yank he found a watch, a notebook, and some folded papers. The notebook and papers he gave to his teacher.

The body he had rifled was Dahlgren's. The papers bore notes like: *Kill Jeff Davis and his cabinet.*

President Lincoln and General Kilpatrick claimed the papers were forged. President Davis and General Lee believed them genuine. The controversy rages to this day.

One fact, though, was clear on the spot. If statesmen were now targets for murder, then the war had become total. There were no knightly rules any longer. There were no rules at all.

The blond colonel who had ridden off so full of life and graceful, thrusting splendor finished in a muddy grave at the fork of two roads. His papers went to Richmond. So did his wooden leg.

The "Dahlgren papers" were eventually lodged in the National Archives. The wooden leg was put briefly on view in a Richmond shop window; afterward it was fitted to John Ballard, one of Mosby's rangers.

Someone unknown got Dahlgren's left little finger, apparently for the ring on it.

ULRIC DAHLGREN

BORN: Pennsylvania, 1842.
DIED: Mantapike Hill, Virginia, March 2, 1864.

THE ILLUSTRATION, PAGE 153: *The ambush of Lieutenant Dahlgren.*

Nathan Bedford Forrest
Lieutenant General, Confederate States of America

37

FASCINATING UPSTART

IN APRIL of 1864 there occurred in the village of Florence, Alabama, one of the most remarkable victories of the war.

During the night one hundred and fifty Confederate infantrymen attacked a much larger body of Union cavalry. As they charged, the Confederates shouted the name of a man who wasn't within a hundred miles.

Their cry bounded through the night. "Forrest! Forrest!"

The Yanks threw up their hands. All resistance had been scared out of them.

The very name of Forrest is a host in itself, one soldier noted gleefully in his diary that night.

Whether in person or by proxy, Nathan Bedford Forrest fought the Union forces in the West with the same result: victory. A born soldier, he understood war with ruthless honesty. "War means fightin' and fightin' means killin'," he said. And no one ever fought and killed more efficiently than this onetime Memphis slave trader.

He was the only man in either army to enter a private and be discharged a lieutenant general. As a colonel he escaped with most of his command from Fort Donelson when it surrendered to Grant. As a brigadier general he served in Kentucky under Braxton Bragg, and as a major general in northern Mississippi and Tennessee. In the last year of the war he commanded the Confederate cavalry in Alabama, Mississippi, and eastern Louisiana.

In the beginning he knew nothing about military practices. He could not even drill the men of his brigade. Yet he won a brilliant little victory at Sacramento, Kentucky, his first battle. He disposed his troops, maneuvered, and timed his counter blow with an instinct that amounted to genius. Not until the Confederacy was ravaged of shelter, food, and hope did he meet defeat.

He was as trimmed for war as a trigger. Frequently he unlimbered his guns right at the skirmish line. In another commander this would have been downright lunacy. Forrest made it pay off again and again.

He coined the phrase, "First with the most," though the way he said it was, "Git thar fust with the most." Seldom did he have the "most" in guns or men.

But he hit the enemy's weak point, and so got into the crucial spot with superior numbers.

He attacked and attacked and attacked. Only in the last weeks, with his men hungry and his horses dying, did he dig in and defend.

In manner he was mild, soft-spoken, and gentle until aroused in battle or irked by a superior officer. "If you ever again try to cross my path it will be at the peril of your life," he once warned General Bragg.

After General Joseph Wheeler had ordered him into a bloody assault on Fort Donelson, Forrest told Wheeler he would never take orders from him again. He never did.

In that assault, Forrest had two horses killed under him, two of twenty-nine he was to lose all told in the saddle. He fought more hand-to-hand duels than any general in any war: his courage was a throwback to the days of Attila.

A mature man in his forties, Forrest had none of the warped indifference to danger that young George Custer had. He did not need Wade Hampton's strength of will, or Jeb Stuart's gallant heart. He used courage naturally, as a pistol uses powder—to strike a target.

He detested a coward. His officers were under orders to shoot any trooper

158

who wavered. Once he dismounted and savagely beat with a stick a man who had slunk off. At Murfreesboro, Tennessee, he shot down the color-bearer of a panicked regiment. Then he picked up the standard and rallied the troops.

General William T. Sherman promised promotion to the Union brigadier who slew Forrest. "It must be done if it costs ten thousand lives and breaks the Treasury," wrote Sherman.

The man valued at ten thousand Yankees looked as if he might be very hard to take, dead or alive. Six feet two inches tall, he possessed powerful, tireless muscles. Something of the clawing determination of his youth showed in his fiercely beautiful face.

His father died when he was sixteen, and he had to help his mother support five brothers and three sisters. Working at first as a farm hand, he shifted to horse- and cattle-trading, and then to dealing in slaves and real estate. He managed his money shrewdly and bought plantations in Mississippi and Arkansas. When he enlisted in the Confederate Army, he was worth a million dollars.

❧

FOR MISSIONS requiring quick and independent thinking, Forrest had no close rival. In boldness he outshone the raider John Morgan. His tactical sense developed beyond Jeb Stuart and Wade Hampton. He rode around and through a procession of good Union cavalry commanders.

In April, 1863, Colonel A. D. Streight stole a page from Forrest's book. The Union officer led one of the early raids into Alabama and Georgia, destroying railroads and supplies.

Forrest, with twelve hundred men, pursued Streight for five days and finally forced him into a conference. The Confederate stood with his back to a cutoff in the road. While the parley ensued, the three pieces of his artillery passed in and out of sight, going round and round. Streight, though he outnumbered Forrest, grew fearful.

"Name of God! How many guns have you got?" he exclaimed. "There's fifteen I've counted already!"

Casually, Forrest turned his head. "I reckon that's all that has kept up," he drawled.

Streight surrendered.

The aristocrats who ran the army back East viewed Forrest with something akin to embarrassment. The ex-private kept winning battles according to his own rules.

And he smacked of the slave market. Except for six months of schooling, he was self-educated. He said "fit" for "fought." "Fetch up," "betwixt," and "reckon" peppered his speech. As a writer, he dropped unnecessary words and letters: Headquarters in the saddle became *Hed Quarters in Sadle*.

The men in Richmond did not quite know how to use this fascinating upstart. President Davis guardedly termed him a "bold and enterprising raider and rider."

All Forrest could do was beat the Yankees. He made the most of what he had. But he did not have what *really* counted, a West Point background.

So he was held to a division until the blood had all seeped from the Confederacy. What if he had been given an army in 1863, when Confederate might stood at the full?

That is the burning question of the war.

NATHAN BEDFORD FORREST

BORN: Chapel Hill, Tennessee, July 13, 1821.
DIED: Memphis, Tennessee, October 29, 1877.

THE ILLUSTRATION, PAGE 157: *Confederate swords.*

SECTION OF THE BRACKET DAM   CRIB OF STONE AND BRICK   SECTION OF THE TREE DAM

Joseph Bailey
Major General, United States of America

38

WOE AT RED RIVER

THE RED RIVER originates in Texas, slices through Arkansas, and empties in Louisiana. It rises and falls without regard to men or wars. In the spring of 1864 the river fell, and thereby piled fresh woes upon a Union expedition already overloaded with bungling and defeat.

General Grant objected to the campaign from the first. The government, however, wanted control of Louisiana and eastern Texas. So in March, 1864, a combined military and naval expedition was launched.

The campaign was still young when Lincoln predicted failure. When it was dead and buried, General Sherman called the business "a blunder from beginning to end."

Not a single commanding officer added to his prestige. One man alone got out a hero. He was Joseph Bailey, who did not fire a shot.

In the upside-down logic of the Red River campaign, it followed that Bailey, an Army officer from an inland town, Salem, Ohio, should save the Navy from sinking its own ships.

161

The Union forces moved in three converging columns under General Nathaniel Banks and his two "insubordinates," General A. J. Smith and General Frederick Steele.

Smith scoffed at political generals like Banks. When told Banks was summoning reserves, he growled, "The fellow already has more men than he knows how to handle!"

Steele was supposed to bring fifteen thousand men down from Arkansas. He brought half the number and harassed Banks worse than the enemy.

The Confederates had only one commander and no quarreling. General E. Kirby Smith literally rolled up Banks at Sabine Cross Roads and then bloodied A. J. Smith at Pleasant Hill. Banks deemed it wise to pack up and go home.

As the Union soldiers retreated along the river road, the guns of Admiral David Porter's fleet laid down protecting salvos. Then Porter ran into troubles of his own.

He had cooperated in the campaign only after being assured the Red River would be navigable. For twenty years it had risen in the spring. This year, while nearby rivers rose on schedule, the Red River sank six feet. Since the voyage upriver a month before, the water had dropped to a mere three feet. At the double falls above Alexandria, ugly boulders poked above the surface.

Porter had left seven gunboats and the largest transports below the falls. The obvious step now was to scuttle the trapped ships and board the ones downriver.

Enter Joseph Bailey, a big, rawboned lieutenant colonel in the 4th Wisconsin.

Bailey's idea was to build a wing dam just above the lower of the two rapids. The dam would back up the water sufficiently to float the ships over the rocks. The year before Bailey had freed two mud-bound Confederate transports by similar means.

Engineers of the Regular Army and Navy had misgivings. Although Bailey had done some civil construction in peacetime, his career had been mainly in lumbering.

"If damning the river would do any good, we should have been out of this long ago," punned doubting Porter.

The pun could not remove the stain threatening Porter's record. Rather than lose most of his fleet without a struggle, he let the landlubber build his dam.

"We have rations only for three weeks," he warned Bailey. "You'll have to bring the water to seven feet in that time."

On may 1, 1864, Bailey began building out from the left bank. The sections of the dam were heavy trees cross-tied with logs. The right bank was almost bare of trees. So the sections from that side were formed of log cribs filled with whatever material the neighborhood yielded. Four coal barges were sunk in midstream to narrow the space between the wing tips.

Bailey had the whole army for a construction gang. Probably no other lieutenant colonel ever commanded so many thousands of soldiers (and sailors) at one time. Actually, he depended chiefly on a few skilled lumbermen from Maine and Wisconsin.

The mass of the soldiers wrestled the sections into the water or scoured the countryside for materials. Buildings were knocked down and a whole mill carted away. Wood, bricks, stones, and machinery were fed into the cribs.

Work was pushed night and day, despite enemy sharpshooters, a boiling sun, and a nine-mile-an-hour current that constantly threatened to wash away the sections. Bailey overcame these handicaps by his own example. He waded in, joked, splashed, and inspired his men to toil like beavers. And what he got looked crazily like the tangled woodwork of those eager little creatures.

On the ninth day, as the wings neared completion, catastrophe struck. Two of the coal barges were dislodged by the current and thrown against the rocks. Precious water poured through the gap.

Quickly Admiral Porter galloped upriver and ordered the ships to run the rapids while there was still enough draft. Thirty thousand soldiers lined the shore to watch the attempt.

The *Lexington* was first. She started boldly, slowed, and then charged into the channel above the long, thirteen-foot drop. At full speed she plunged into churning water. Her bow smacked hard, fanning spray high on either side. She leveled off, skimmed the rocks, and passed safely into the quiet waters below. The *Fort Hindman*, *Osage*, and *Neosho* followed as the soldiers yelled like Indians.

But the water was leaking out too swiftly. Rocks appeared. Six gunboats and two tugs were still marooned.

Bailey now did the impossible. In three days and three nights he built three more wing dams, just above the upper rapids. The water rose fourteen inches above the highest previous mark. On May 12 and 13 the remaining ships passed through.

"It would have taken a private company a year to do what you did in twelve days," asserted Admiral Porter, as he gratefully presented Bailey with a sword.

The officers of the fleet added a purse of three thousand dollars. Congress granted a vote of thanks.

Bailey was promoted to brigadier general and eventually to brevet major general. The war over, he settled in Vernon County, Missouri, and was elected sheriff.

He was shot to death two years later by two bushwhackers he was bringing back to jail.

JOSEPH BAILEY

> BORN: Pennsville, Ohio, May 6, 1825.
> DIED: Vernon County, Missouri, March 21, 1867.

THE ILLUSTRATION, PAGE 161: *Red River Dam, with the "Lexington" running the rapids.*

La Fayette Curry Baker
Brigadier General, United States of America

39

SECRET SERVICE TYRANT

IN ROOM 17 of Barnum's Hotel in Baltimore, Maryland, two men sat sizing each other up. The plump man was A. E. Ackney. His card described him as a hardware dealer of Philadelphia.

The other man was short and lean. He had a light brown beard and strange, searching gray eyes. He called himself Mr. Munson.

"Mr. Ackney, I'm a man of very few words," he said, breaking the silence. "I'm an agent of the Confederate Government, and I understand you are willing to help us. I want to purchase goods, and I have the gold to pay for them."

The word *gold* had a pleasant, solid tone. Confederate paper money was showing worrisome frailty.

"I may be able to help you," admitted Ackney.

"I'd like some proof," said Munson. "I have to be careful."

"Of course." Ackney took out an envelope. It contained two contracts.

One was to furnish a Northern regiment with oats and hay. The other was to supply the South with arms.

"I have a boat on the river," Ackney said slyly. "We fill the hold with small arms and cover it with forage. We unload the arms at Matthias Point and then land the forage in Washington. I help the South, and make a little money out of the North in the bargain."

Munson glared. "I don't want to make a cent out of this business for myself," he announced coldly.

"That is honorable and patriotic," Ackney hurried to agree. "But it's not safe to buy goods here. The police watch us all the time. We can do better in Philadelphia."

In Philadelphia, Ackney's cronies checked Munson's papers, and a deal was closed. But before Munson could show his bag of gold, the police swooped down. Seized with the traitors was a quarter million dollars in cannon-primers, friction caps, rifles, and pistols.

Munson did not go to prison with the others. He dropped his phony Southern accent, returned to Washington, and resumed his identity as La Fayette Baker, Union spy.

Baker's talent for deception, his daring, and his results were duly noted by his superiors. As yet, the driving interest of Baker in Baker had not clearly emerged. But the day was not too distant when men explained the success of this exmechanic by the old saying, "Set a rogue to catch a rogue."

Baker bagged rogues, male and female, by the score. In Philadelphia, he had discovered one of life's great thrills—power. Operating as a secret agent of the State Department, he went on to make arrests in Washington, Baltimore, and southern Maryland, which were the main areas of illegal trade with the Confederacy. Then he arrested a prominent New York editor without a warrant. He had overreached himself. Newspapers screamed for his removal.

The State Department dumped him. That same afternoon he walked into the office of the Secretary of War, Edwin Stanton.

At this time detectives attached to the army worked for individual generals. None knew what the others were doing. The system was wasteful. Baker proposed to reorganize the secret service into a central agency.

"With you as chief?" inquired Stanton, smiling shrewdly.

"Naturally," replied Baker, and added with equal shrewdness, "I would be answerable to you, Mr. Secretary."

Stanton turned down the plea. Nevertheless, he was impressed by the intense little man with the strange, restless gray eyes, and took him on as a special agent. In a few months Baker got results that banished certain doubts. Stanton gave him full rein.

Baker became a provost marshal of the War Department with the rank of colonel. His powers were so ill-defined as to be almost limitless. He called his organization the National Detective Bureau. Starting with ten agents, he hired men at a furious speed. Their main qualification was loyalty to La Fayette Baker.

By the end of the war he could brag: "There are two thousand secret agents reporting to me."

❦

IN THE BEGINNING the people of Washington were full of his praise. What if his methods were a trifle high-handed? He was cleaning out the law-breakers.

Baker's bully boys pursued traitors, counterfeiters, speculators, and bounty jumpers. They seized illegal supplies of medicine and drugs and jailed stewards and nurses who robbed in hospitals. On the subject of gambling and whisky, Baker's righteous anger glowed white hot.

Abraham Lincoln was among the first to see the power-hungry detective clearly. One day a resident of Washington complained to the President that a man disturbed him by grinding a hand organ in front of his home.

Counseled Lincoln: "Speak to Stanton about it, and tell him to send Baker after the man. Baker will steal the organ and throw its owner into the Old Capitol Prison."

By 1864 there was more truth than humor in the President's remark. The very mention of Baker's name could quiet a room. In three short years he had risen from a harmless nobody to become America's most feared man.

Day and night suspects filed into his office in the basement of the Treasury Building. Some were held and questioned for weeks. If anyone demanded lawful treatment, he was spirited to the Old Capitol Prison where no civil authority could help him. Lincoln had suspended *habeas corpus* for the war, and Baker traded craftily on this loss of personal rights.

"To save the Union, you have to get tough," he insisted. While saving the Union, he ignored writs, imprisoned hundreds, and stole thousands of dollars.

"In my job, I'm bound to make enemies," he told Stanton. An old hand at enemy-making, Stanton disregarded the cries of "thief," "tyrant," and "liar" hurled at his hatchetman.

Baker's reign of terror seemed secure for years—until a newspaper exposed him as a bribe taker and blackmailer. As his foes closed in, John Wilkes Booth murdered Lincoln. Stanton summoned Baker to find the assassin, and Baker did.

He enjoyed a brief comeback as the nation's hero. It ended when the scandals of his office were revived. Congress cut his share of the Booth reward from $17,500 to $3,750. When several National Detective Bureau agents were discovered snooping in the White House, President Johnson removed him for good.

Baker made one last bid to reinstate himself. As the star witness against President Johnson at the impeachment action, he tried to link the chief executive to the Booth plot. The "proof" he threatened to introduce somehow never materialized.

Disgraced and friendless, Baker retired to Philadelphia. A year before his death in 1868 he completed a book, *History of the Secret Service*. It is, unsurprisingly, a conscienceless mixture of fact and fable.

LA FAYETTE CURRY BAKER

BORN: Stafford, New York, October 13, 1826.
DIED: Philadelphia, Pennsylvania, July 3, 1868.

THE ILLUSTRATION, PAGE 165: *The Old Capitol prison.*

Jubal Anderson Early
Lieutenant General, Confederate States of America

40

THE BAD OLD MAN

JUBAL EARLY slouched forward in his saddle, his forearm resting on the pommel, his black eyes intent and glowing. Six miles away lay the plumpest prize of three years of war—the city of Washington.

Old Jube could hear the church bells pealing. Their message of alarm floated above empty garrisons. General Grant had called practically every able-bodied soldier down to Petersburg, Virginia, where Lee was holed up. And while Grant laid siege, Lee had sent Early boldly up to the Union's unguarded front door.

Early's orders were to threaten, not to storm. But snarling Old Jube had ten thousand men and ideas of his own. If he could drive into the feebly defended city, take Abraham Lincoln prisoner, burn and loot—

The buildings sprawled white and unscarred in the hot noon sun. They contrasted sharply with the bullet-pocked houses of Virginia. Old Jube, hunched by rheumatism and embittered by Yankees, hankered to rain punishment on all that Northern sleekness.

As a former county prosecutor, he had had a thorough grounding in the

169

benefits of "an eye for an eye." To him all Yankees were squirmy criminals. Not without some cause did Lee, jokingly, call him "my bad old man."

Early spat a jet of tobacco juice, pulled his gaze from the Capitol dome, and galloped southward along the Seventh Street pike. Before Fort Stevens, one of the gates to the city, he raised his field glasses. The redoubts looked weakly manned.

"Your mission is to demonstrate, to draw off some of Grant's troops," Lee had told him. Early took another look at Fort Stevens. "Go in," he ordered Major General Robert Rodes.

Every minute counted. Intelligence reports had two crack enemy corps traveling up the Potomac as fast as paddle wheels could spin.

Even as he watched Rodes's skirmishers advance, Old Jube spied a column of dust moving toward the fort. Bluecoats filed into the works. Soon heavy artillery began roaring.

He recalled the attack. He could not risk losing men. As dust settled, he sent cavalry to probe for another way through the forts that girded the city.

That night—July 11, 1864—the Confederates held a council of war. Meanwhile, Union troops arrived to strengthen the defenses of the capital.

At daylight, Early attacked. When things did not go as expected, he rode to the front. The parapets were lined with Yankees. He stopped the assault.

If Old Jube had arrived a day sooner, he could have marched into a city protected only by militiamen, clerks, and convalescents. The Confederate flag would have flown above the Capitol dome. Confederate wagons would have creaked with the gold and silver of the United States Treasury.

Twenty-four hours had denied Jubal Early a pedestal beside Lee and Jackson. The high tide of the Confederacy had risen, and now the gaunt Gray columns ebbed. Washington stood unscathed.

Old Jube was not through, however. The hardbitten, forty-eight-year-old bachelor had been rebuffed, and he tended to get "ornery as a bearcat" when that happened. In his strongboxes was $220,000, tributes exacted from Hagerstown and Frederick on the route to Washington. He craved more. He pounded into Pennsylvania to get it.

Chambersburg, a town of six thousand, had twice been robbed of horses, wagons, and grain. Jeb Stuart had raided it in 1862. Lee had gathered his army there for the assault upon Gettysburg in 1863. Stuart and Lee were angels of mercy compared to Early in 1864.

At 6:00 A.M. on a sleepy Saturday four guns spoke from the hills. Immediately thereafter Early's cavalry swarmed into the town. Brigadier General John McCausland delivered an ultimatum to citizens caught on the streets.

Pay half a million dollars in greenbacks or one hundred thousand in gold within half an hour. If not, Chambersburg is ashes blowing in the wind.

There wasn't that much money in the town. McCausland patiently abided by the half hour's grace. Then men in butternut darted in and out, setting fires.

The houses were cotton dry, as the past two weeks had been rainless. Fifteen minutes after the first spiral of smoke appeared, the main part of town resounded with the crackling of timbers and the crash of falling walls.

Early's grim men trotted away. Behind them smoke spread out in the sky like "a sackcloth over the doomed city." Two-thirds of Chambersburg collapsed in blackened ruins.

᷎

THE LEVELING of Chambersburg, a town without military importance, outraged the North. Grant gave Philip Sheridan fifty thousand soldiers and orders to follow Early to the death.

Sheridan moved into Early's nest, the Shenandoah Valley of Virginia. Thus began an eight-month duel between two soldiers who, unaided by family connections, had climbed to the rank of major general, and would climb higher.

Fortune jilted Jube. He disliked cavalry, yet the area was open country favorable to mounted warfare. He had only two thousand horsemen, but half of these had no sabers and so could not fight to advantage. He faced a typically superior force; untypically, the Union commander was not bogged down by his own weight.

Jube, full of vinegar and bluff, outfoxed Sheridan until the Valley harvest was reaped and transported south.

In September Sheridan finally overtook him and whipped him twice. But Jube rebounded and nearly stole a victory at Cedar Creek in mid-October. His starving soldiers let go of pursuit to dip both hands into the rich Federal camps. While they sat down and feasted, Sheridan, riding from Winchester twenty miles away, rallied his fugitives to victory.

The final chapter was written March 2, 1865. Only a remnant—one thousand men and six guns—remained of Jube's army. Sheridan brushed into him at Waynesboro. Early pitched to the fight, but it was over quickly.

Sheridan's legions squashed him underfoot. With twenty men Jube escaped to Petersburg and reported the disaster to Lee. Because of strong public opinion, Lee reluctantly withheld another command from his "bad old man."

A month later came Appomattox.

Old Jube, still snarling, went to Mexico, thence to Cuba and Canada rather than "submit to the rule of our enemies."

Although he returned to this country, he refused to swear loyalty to the United States. To his death he remained "unreconstructed."

JUBAL ANDERSON EARLY

BORN: Franklin County, Virginia, November 3, 1816.
DIED: Lynchburg, Virginia, March 2, 1894.

THE ILLUSTRATION, PAGE 169: *Reinforcements manning gun at Fort Stevens, Washington, D. C., July, 1864.*

Philip Henry Sheridan
Major General, United States of America

41

FROM TWENTY MILES AWAY

"DRESS RIGHT!" the command rang across the parade grounds at West Point.

In the opinion of the cadet sergeant the snap of a bandy-legged little youth had been less than model. The offender, Philip Sheridan, was chewed out and ordered to try once more. Sheridan objected, and soon hot words were flying.

Up and over boiled Sheridan's temper. He lowered his bayonet and lunged forward. Fortunately, his better judgment checked him. The point stopped a fraction shy of contact.

The harm was done, however. The cadet sergeant reported the incident, as required by Academy rules.

Sheridan had all that night to brood. He had set his heart upon becoming an officer. West Point, he was discovering, wasn't everything he dreamed it would be. He was from a small, friendly town; the social life at the Academy was impersonal, aloof. He was a Northerner, the son of poor Irish immigrants; the Academy was dominated by aristocratic Southerners. Topping these handicaps was his appearance. He stood five feet five inches, with long arms and short, bowed legs. In the stiff, tight cadet uniform he looked like the mascot.

Sheridan felt he had been unjustly picked on by the cadet sergeant, a big Virginian named William Terrill. By morning he was positive of it. He greeted Terrill outside the barracks with fists swinging.

Sheridan was getting soundly drubbed—though he was far from quitting—when an officer intervened. Letters of explanation were demanded of both youths. For his breach of discipline, Sheridan was suspended a year.

He spent the enforced vacation working at Finck & Dittoe's dry-goods store in his home town. He returned for his final year at West Point a good deal wiser. Henceforth, he did his fist-fighting where officers were not likely to pass.

These out-of-the-way brawls were not altogether private. Word of them reached the Academic Board. Demerits piled up. On graduation day, Sheridan teetered within five demerits of being expelled.

Once free of the Academy's spit-and-polish, Phil Sheridan's fighting spirit ought to have instantly distinguished him as a soldier. Such was not the case. Although he did his duty capably against the Indians in the Northwest, he was out of step in the peacetime army.

Garrison life fitted him poorly. He had no outside income with which to indulge his pleasures or entertain his comrades. He did not make friends readily. He refused to bootlick his superiors. In a society where good manners often counted more than the call of duty, he committed a coarse error: he clung to the conviction that he was as good as any man.

For eight years he remained a lieutenant. In the spring of 1861 he received his promotion to captain. His war service started in the quartermaster corps in Missouri.

He handled paperwork by the ton, thirsted for action, and acquired a reputation for thoroughness. In May, 1862 he jumped from captain in the Regular Army to colonel of volunteers, commanding the 2nd Michigan Cavalry. With a combat assignment, his journey to greatness began.

The troopers who had their first look at Colonel Sheridan were surprised. He appeared more like a tough little sergeant than "an officer and gentleman."

They promptly learned what he was: a professional soldier with no frills and no swagger. He knew how to use horses.

He moved them faster and got them to the enemy fresher than anyone in the West. He had a habit of studying the land, and he never turned in at night without knowing the weakness and strength of every yard around him. He saved his men from unnecessary toil and got results in battle. His methods and quiet self-confidence inspired everyone around him.

Victory followed victory. A little more than a month after he'd been promoted from desk captain, Phil Sheridan won his brigadier general's star.

When U. S. Grant took over the Army of the Potomac, he brought Sheridan East and gave him the cavalry corps. Neither President Lincoln nor Secretary of War Stanton was much impressed with "Little Phil." But they went along with Grant.

Stanton thought Sheridan too young (he was thirty-three). Lincoln, standing a head taller, hoped he would "fulfill the expectations of General Grant."

Sheridan reorganized the cavalry from top to bottom, and in a month took it on the warpath with Grant. Success assured him his troopers could whip the Gray cavalry if given the chance. To prove his boast, Grant let him go after Jeb Stuart, the gallant Confederate leader.

In seven days Sheridan's grinding power battered aside the weakened Gray horsemen and killed Stuart. The Confederacy never recovered from the loss.

᪐

IN AUGUST, 1864, Sheridan got his biggest assignment. For three years Virginia's fertile Shenandoah Valley had supported Confederate troops that had defeated the Union armies again and again. Grant wanted the Valley knocked out of the war.

Sheridan laid waste to the region. He thrashed crusty Jubal Early at Winchester and Fisher's Hill. "Old Jube" bounced back. While Sheridan was returning from a conference in Washington, Early attacked at Cedar Creek.

Twenty miles off, Sheridan heard the artillery. He rode to the battlefield and saw his men in retreat. Up and down his army he tore, waving his hat and shouting, "About face, boys! We're going back. We're going to lick them out of their boots."

The sight of the fighting little general on his big black horse rallied the dazed soldiers. Everybody and everything turned around and followed Sheridan. By late afternoon, the Confederates were routed. The Valley was knocked out of the war for good.

"This Sheridan," declared Lincoln, "is a little Irishman, but he is a big fighter."

At the defeat of the South, Sheridan was the nation's number three soldier. Ahead of him in public favor stood only Grant and Sherman.

The scrappy youth who barely was permitted to graduate West Point eventually became commander in chief of the United States Army. Two months before his death on August 5, 1888, he was granted the highest military rank, that of full general.

His widow, though still youthful and pretty, never remarried. When asked why she did not, she is supposed to have answered: "I would rather be the widow of Philip Sheridan than the wife of any man living."

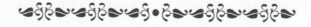

PHILIP HENRY SHERIDAN

> BORN: Albany, New York, March 6, 1831.
> DIED: Nonquitt, Massachusetts, August 5, 1888.

THE ILLUSTRATION, PAGE 173: *Sheridan and his Winchester charger.*

Bennett Henderson Young
Lieutenant, Confederate States of America

42

VERMONT RAID

AFTER THREE YEARS of war, nobody in St. Albans had yet glimpsed a Confederate soldier.

This was hardly remarkable. The little Vermont town nestled far in the north, just fifteen miles below the Canadian border. Few communities in the entire Union had less reason to worry about seeing the enemy.

Only Emma Sedwell had a foreboding.

"I dreamed it again," she told her husband on the morning of October 19, 1864. "The streets were full of Rebels."

John Sedwell laughed. His wife read too many illustrated weeklies. "Any Reb this far north would freeze to death. Besides, what would they want up here?"

While Sedwell scoffed at his wife's foolishness, Lieutenant Bennett Young paced the floor two blocks away. Young had not slept too well, either.

From his "headquarters" in Room 23 of the Tremont House, he stared down at the main street of the little Yankee town. "Whatever happens," he told himself, "it will all be over by dusk."

177

The gangling cavalryman was not ordinarily a worrier. You couldn't be the jittery kind and ride with John Morgan—ride, that is, until the general had brashly galloped into Ohio and got captured. Young had broken out of Camp Douglas, near Chicago, and escaped into Canada.

Now the twenty-one-year-old officer had a command, twenty other exprisoners. They composed the northernmost outpost of the Confederate Army.

There was a light knock on the door. Before Young could answer, one of his men, Dan Butterworth, came in.

"Moore and Swager are for cutting the telegraph wires," said Butterworth. "They're afraid the bluecoats might be down on us before we can light out."

"The telegraph stays up," replied Young tartly.

The wires were essential to the aftermath of the raid. When they hummed with the news that the United States had been invaded by looters, Washington would be thrown into a panic. To calm towns along the Canadian border, troops would be withdrawn from the front, giving Confederate forces everywhere a breathing spell.

"We're not only going after their money," reminded Young, strapping on a pair of Navy six-shooters. "We're going to pay them back for a lot of ruined towns and farms in Dixie."

The other Confederates were on the streets. Under their coats were six-shooters like Young's. As they strolled they were greeted by a few of the townsfolk who knew them as members of a Canadian sports club. The young "sportsmen" had been assembling in St. Albans for ten days. They planned a "fishing trip to Lake Champlain."

A church clock chimed three. Suddenly the fishermen shed their overcoats and unholstered their sixes.

"In the name of the Confederate States of America," hollered Young, standing spread-legged in front of his hotel, "I take possession of St. Albans!"

People stopped and gaped. A few hooted at the armed stranger in the lumberman's shirt and brown kersey cloth trousers. The jibes and chuckles changed to gasps when Young put holes through two hats.

"Everybody off the street," he ordered.

His raiders went smoothly into action. Three squads entered the three St. Albans banks to clean out all the money for the Confederate treasury. Another squad began moving the crowd toward the square. Another rounded up horses, and still another set about shattering fifty bottles of Greek Fire against designated buildings in the center of town.

❧

Of the five thousand people in St. Albans, John Sedwell was the first to realize the unbelievable was really happening. As a teller in the Franklin County Bank, he beheld his wife's nightmare replayed at gunpoint. Two raiders compelled him to stack a hundred thousand dollars in their bags.

As smoke puffed from windows, the crowd began to mutter and stir. Against a backdrop of make-believe, a few hard facts popped out: the burning houses, the occasional shots, the tall figure of Young standing in his stirrups as he rode up and down Main Street.

Young's attention was rapidly focusing on the getaway.

"More horses," he shouted. "Get more horses!" Mounts were led from Fuller's Livery Stable and commandeered from farmers' wagons.

A rifle cracked. Young twisted in the saddle and fired back. Glass crashed onto the street. Men from the outskirts of town were running to the trouble, carrying rifles. A full-sized skirmish was developing. One citizen, Henry Watson, a tailor, was killed. Three raiders were wounded.

In the telegraph office an operator fumblingly tapped out a message to Governor John Gregory Smith:

Southern raiders are in St. Albans shooting citizens, burning houses.

The message was relayed to Washington. Abraham Lincoln was awaiting news of the battle at Cedar Creek, Virginia. Instead he heard an amazing report. A Confederate army was sweeping down from Canada. St. Albans, Vermont, was already occupied.

For forty-five minutes the town was controlled by the Confederates.

Young roared: "Move out!" and the raiders swung into the saddle. By a huge elm opposite the city hall, the last shots were exchanged. Elinas Morrison was slain and another townsman wounded.

With two hundred thousand dollars of United States currency stowed in their haversacks, the raiders galloped for the Canadian border. At Black Creek, they fired a hay wagon and pushed it to the middle of a covered bridge. The bridge burned, foiling pursuit.

Eventually Young and five of his men were arrested by Canadian authorities and tried in Montreal. Canadian opinion being sympathetic to them, they were released. Canada repaid the

St. Albans banks fifty thousand dollars. The remainder of the cash and securities was never recovered.

So the raid netted money and damaged property. But it failed in the big job of drawing Yankee troops up to protect the towns strung along the Canadian border. The pressure on Lee continued unrelieved.

Yet Bennett Young and his handful of daredevils had worked a subtle and enduring change. The people of the North did not lie down in bed at night without first glancing out the window and, for a moment, listening.

After St. Albans, the Confederates were never more than a hoofbeat from Main Street, U.S.A.

BENNETT HENDERSON YOUNG

BORN: Nicholasville, Kentucky, May 25, 1843.
DIED: Louisville, Kentucky, February 23, 1919.

THE ILLUSTRATION, PAGE 177: *The Bank in St. Albans, Vt. at time of the Confederate raid.*

William Barker Cushing
Lieutenant, United States of America

43

TORPEDO MAN

IN MAY, 1864, the United States Navy had a job for a man who enjoyed risking his neck.

A new Confederate ironclad, the *Albemarle*, said to be more powerful than the *Merrimack*, ruled the inland waters of North Carolina. The wooden ships of the Union fleet were no match for her. The Union ironclads, which drew too much water, could not reach her.

The only way to destroy the *Albemarle* was to blow her up. That meant a sneak raid, led by an experienced officer.

The Navy foresaw one hitch. Probably none of the raiding party would survive.

Acting Rear Admiral S. P. Lee, commanding the North Atlantic Squadron, had just the man to lead the expedition —a nerveless six-footer named William Cushing.

In 1861, Will Cushing had been dismissed from the Naval Academy, largely because of repeated squabbles with his Spanish professor. Shifting for himself, he had won advancement faster than his exclassmates.

"Where there is danger in battle,

there I will be, for I will gain a name in this war," he had vowed. By seeking danger, he had jumped from master's mate to lieutenant. At nineteen, he was the youngest man to hold that rank.

Small boat raids were Will's specialty. He worked out a simple, bold plan, had it approved, and began at once to move toward his rendezvous with the *Albemarle*.

On October 23, the young lieutenant arrived at Roanoke Island, a Union stronghold. There he received bad news. A newspaper had printed his plan for the destruction of the ironclad. Although incorrect in some details, the account would certainly tighten the Confederate defenses.

Undaunted, Will steamed up the Roanoke River to where the Union fleet kept uneasy watch for the *Albemarle*. The ironclad was moored eight miles upriver at Plymouth. On the night of October 26, Will and twenty volunteers shoved off in a launch and a cutter.

They quickly turned back. The motor of the launch chugged so noisily the enemy would be warned a mile away. Will had a ship's carpenter muffle the engine with a wooden box wrapped in tarpaulin.

The next night, at 11:28, the party started out again. The first obstacle lay a mile below the *Albemarle*. This was the wreck of the Union ship *Southfield*. The task of the thirteen men in the cutter was to leap aboard the wreck and subdue the Confederate guards stationed there before they could fire a signal rocket.

Slowly the launch plugged upstream. The men huddled tensely in the darkness. It would take two hours to reach the ironclad, and strict silence was essential.

One of the seamen suddenly began to cough. An officer muffled him in his coat. "Good for you, Mr. Howorth," whispered Will.

"I'll muffle you up, sir, if you say another word," threatened the dutiful Howorth.

Will smiled and peered into the darkness. It was past two o'clock. They ought to be at the *Southfield* soon . . .

᷐᪵

Almost with this thought came the sight of the wreck. Steadily the launch drew closer. The raiders could hear the voices of the sentries in the blackness. It seemed impossible that the Rebels did not hear, from twenty yards off, the gurgle of water about the two prows, the low throb of the muffled engine.

The men in the cutter sat with oars poised. At the first hail, they would cast free of the launch and spring into action. Time dragged by. The voices faded. The launch pulled safely around a bend in the river.

Ahead now was the big one. Will stared into the rainy night. Ten minutes slipped away. Then, at 3:00 A.M., he had a look at the *Albemarle*. She stood out from the faintly lighted sky as a huge square mass.

The launch puffed onward. On the shore at Plymouth were four thousand Confederate soldiers. Neither they nor the crew of the *Albemarle* were aware of the handful of men gliding into their midst.

In a spurt of reckless enthusiasm, Will determined to board the ironclad and pirate her. But a dog barked. A drowsy sentry awoke, lifted a musket, and shouted, "Who's there?" When no answer came, the cry was repeated, loudly and nervously.

"Cast off!" hollered Will to the men in the cutter. He ordered them to row back and silence the Rebels on the *Southfield*, thus clearing the escape route. The element of surprise was lost, and with it the chance of capturing the *Albemarle*. She would have to be torpedoed.

The Confederates on ship and shore were hurrying to arms. The launch with its seven Yanks sped for the ironclad.

While still twenty-five yards off, Will saw a chain of cypress logs encircling the sleek black hull—a defense especially designed against a torpedo.

He veered off. Coolly he circled the logs as bullets whizzed about him. There was no way through. He turned the launch wide and headed back at the logs in a dash. Once inside, he knew, he could never muster the speed to get out. He would be penned in with the ironclad.

A volley of buckshot tore the back off his coat and the heel off his shoe. The launch struck the logs, passed half over, and hung with bow quivering in air.

Luckily, Will was close enough to plant the torpedo. Ten feet away, one of the *Albemarle's* hundred-pound rifles pointed at him. It would take twenty seconds, he estimated, for the Confederates to discharge the gun.

Bullets fired at point-blank range from the ironclad ripped his collar and sleeve. Carefully, he worked the torpedo-carrying boom, oblivious to the hail of shot. He pulled the firing-pin line—delicately, so as not to break it.

The torpedo and the hundred-pound rifle exploded together. The gun's charge passed harmlessly over the raiders' heads.

"Surrender, or we'll blow you out of the water!" bellowed a voice from the *Albemarle*.

"Never! I'll be damned first!" Will Cushing yelled, and dived overboard. Three of his crew followed. The others surrendered before the storm of death.

Will made it to shore. The next day he learned the *Albemarle* had sunk to the bottom of the Roanoke River. Before the week was out, he fulfilled his vow: his name was known across the nation, printed in newspaper headlines.

On December 20, 1864, Congress passed a resolution thanking him for his incredible feat.

WILLIAM BARKER CUSHING

BORN: Lake Nemahbin, Wisconsin, November 4, 1842.
DIED: Washington, D. C., December 17, 1874.

THE ILLUSTRATION, PAGE 181: *Cushing's torpedo boat attacking the "Albemarle."*

Abraham Lincoln
President, United States of America

44

THE UNCOMMON MAN

IT WAS EASY to get into the White House. All anyone needed was a note or a word from his Congressman. So the people came. They crowded eight feet from the President of the United States and asked their favors. Because they were the people, the patient, tired man listened.

"My daughter is a genius," insisted a woman. "She has written a story—a hundred and twelve chapters. Will you read it and give me an opinion? And please write a note. It will have weight with the publishers—"

A blank-eyed fellow thundered, "I want you to listen to me! Do exactly as I say, for I have had a vision—"

A motherly lady demanded the government pay for her dead cow. A beautiful girl pleaded for a pass through the lines. A soldier begged for an eight-week furlough.

They came for jobs, commissions, promotions, reprieves from death sentences, pensions. They came every day.

But on November 8, 1864, they did not come. The waiting room outside the President's office was empty. The streets of Washington were nearly deserted. It was Election Day.

A nation tired of war was making a choice. It was deciding whether to re-elect the uncommon man who said a united country was still worth fighting for. And dying for.

At 7:00 P.M., Abraham Lincoln departed the White House with one of his secretaries, John Hay. The night was dark and rainy. The two men sloshed to the War Department to await returns.

The front door was locked. So Lincoln and Hay splashed around to a side door and entered through the Navy Department. Wet and chilled, Lincoln went directly to the telegraph office one flight upstairs.

A batch of telegrams was handed him. Good news from Philadelphia, Baltimore, and Boston. The party's chances had obviously been bolstered by the recent victories of General Sheridan and General Sherman.

Shaking rain from his cloak, Lincoln settled down to the election vigil. Uncertainty and doubt strained in the air. His defeat, he believed, was "exceedingly probable." His speech to George B. McClellan, the Democratic candidate, pledging full support, was already worded.

General Thomas Eckert came in, his trousers caked with mud. While watching another man tumble, he had gone skidding himself. Everyone chuckled to hear him tell it.

Lincoln remarked: "For such an awkward fellow, I am pretty sure-footed. It used to take a pretty dextrous man to throw me."

Thirty-three years earlier he had wrestled the champion of the Clary Grove Boys, a gang of young toughs in New Salem, Illinois. Abe Lincoln not only won the match, but, amazingly, the friendship of the gang. He had an ability to attract the good will of all walks of men. That ability was to take him farther than the strength in his arms.

Early election returns clattered in. They continued favorable. Lincoln had them relayed to his wife. "She is more anxious than I," he said. He was unfailingly thoughtful of the woman who troubled his private life, and who would close her days insane.

The storm affected the working of the telegraph wires. Around ten o'clock a period of silence occurred. The President filled the lull with recollections and anecdotes.

He had a memory for funny stories. He used them to illustrate a point or tilt an argument his way. "This puts me in mind of a story," he would begin.

His friends loved him for his stories, his plain talk, his honesty. Somehow his awkward six feet four inches fitted patly the requirements of unspoiled kindness.

Born in a log cabin, he had risen from humble pursuits: felling trees, splitting rails, keeping store, acting as village postmaster. Often alone, he had found comfort and renewal in solitude. A self-taught lawyer, he had become a shrewd politician but a mediocre Congressman. Later, his debates with Stephen Douglas had spread his name throughout the country. His enemies called him liar, thief, braggart, and swindler.

❧

SOMEWHERE along about 1858, all the pieces seemed to slide into place. The shrewdness and honesty, the sorrow and solitude clasped together. In those first few months as President, cracks appeared here and there. But under the heat and pressure of war, the cracks, instead of widening, fused. The masterpiece that was Abraham Lincoln stood to the world.

He managed the war, the draft, foreign relations, and politics. He freed the slaves and planned the reconstruc-tion of the South. He ruled a Cabinet of brilliant, jealous, ambitious men.

Poised and polished statesmen shrank "instinctively from the contact of a great reality like Lincoln's character," said John Hay.

Evening lengthened into night. At the telegraph office arrived reports from the Western states. By midnight the outcome was certain. Abraham Lincoln had been reelected.

General Eckert provided supper. The President walked to the buffet table with his shambling gait. "Awkwardly and hospitably he went to work shoveling out fried oysters."

It was nearly 2:30 A.M. when he started to leave. The storm had lifted. The night was mild. A brass band and a small group of serenaders summoned him with music and cheers.

He spoke briefly. "It is no pleasure to me to triumph over any one," he said. "But I give thanks to the Almighty for this evidence of the people's resolution to stand by free government and the rights of humanity."

The Almighty entered his utterances frequently, and yet he belonged to no church.

"When any church," he said, "will inscribe over its altar, as its sole qualification for membership . . . *Thou shalt love the Lord thy God with all thy heart, and with all thy soul, and with all thy mind . . . and thy neighbor as thyself,* that church will I join . . ."

Four months after his reelection he was dead, slain by an assassin's bullet. In his years as President, Abraham Lincoln had broadened the destiny of America, and had left behind him a mystery and a heritage.

What deep, mysterious wells were his? From where arose the patience for the favor seekers? The iron strength to bind a nation? The loyalty toward a much talked about wife? The profound beauty of speeches like the Gettysburg address?

In the mysterious grandeur of this backwoods lawyer lies his contribution to the making of America. Abraham Lincoln left to us all the heritage of human majesty.

ABRAHAM LINCOLN

BORN: Hardin County, Kentucky, February 12, 1809.
DIED: Washington, D. C., April 15, 1865.

THE ILLUSTRATION, PAGE 185: *A campaign cartoon of 1864, and a soldier's ballot.*

188

William Tecumseh Sherman
Major General, United States of America

45

THE MARCH TO THE SEA

ON NOVEMBER 15, 1864, some 62,000 Northern soldiers left the flaming city of Atlanta, Georgia, broke all communications, and disappeared for a month.

Foreign military experts wondered if this were the most foolish operation ever attempted, or the most brilliant. Day after day Lincoln and Grant anxiously waited for news of the free-rolling army. And Georgia, feeling the bite of 62,000 soldiers, raised a howl that has sounded to this day.

The man who conceived and led the march was a lean major general with a reddish beard and a harshly lined face —William Tecumseh Sherman.

In him ran strange crosscurrents. He hated war, yet waged it supremely well. He admired the South and had planned to live there, yet he loyally wore the uniform of the North.

From his burning base at Atlanta, he marched eastward toward the coast. Before him stretched fat and unscarred Georgia farms, the Confederacy's last breadbasket. Sherman intended to empty that basket to the bottom. By destroying the means of continuing the war, he would bring a staggering Confederacy crashing to its knees.

His army was trimmed to fighting weight. None but soldiers fit for a long march was in ranks. Ammunition wagons, ambulances, and baggage were pared to a minimum.

Fifteen miles were covered that first day. Once Sherman got off his horse to demonstrate how to use a new invention for ripping up railroad tracks. He was acting the role he had cast for himself.

"The way to be popular with troops is not to be free and familiar with them, but make them believe you know more than they do," he confided to a friend. "My men believe I know everything; they are much mistaken, but it gives them confidence in me."

As he led his army like a plague across Georgia, he maintained the confidence of his men. But there were vital things he didn't know.

In his rear he had left General George Thomas to wreck the Confederate army under John Hood. In his front, Grant had to hold Lee. How were Thomas and Grant faring? If Hood or Lee broke loose, Sherman could expect disaster. He had not enough food or ammunition to engage in a running campaign.

His army could not feed off the land and trade blows with a strong foe besides.

In the morning he was up at four o'clock. He gave orders as if no fears haunted him.

Each brigade sent out a foraging party of twenty or thirty men. By sundown, Northern soldiers were feasting. Veterans used to hardtack and beans stuffed themselves with delicacies that had been at sunup the property of nearby farmers.

Sherman's rules tried to keep foraging within bounds. He forbade any homes to be entered or threatening language spoken. Withal, he drew a nice line between "the rich who are usually hostile," and the hard-working poor, who are "usually neutral or friendly."

Well-stocked barns and pens offered tempting prizes not easily resisted. As the days passed, the foragers grew skilled at their craft. Looting was hard to control among men who had fought the Confederates for three years.

An assortment of wagons and buggies nightly wheeled into camp loaded with "everything . . . a lot of fool soldiers could take in their heads to bring away." The army of 62,000 marched toward the sea in a holiday mood.

There was scant fighting. The slumping Confederate cavalry in Georgia, under Joseph Wheeler, was no match for Sherman's "bummers."

Southern leaders appealed to the population to turn out in their own defense.

"Let every man fly to arms," General Beauregard wired the citizens of Georgia.

The Augusta *Constitutionalist* urged the people to burn their farms. "Let the invader find the desolation he would leave behind staring him in the face."

Across a scorched earth Sherman could not march and survive. His answer was blunt and savage. If the enemy burned forage he would burn Southern houses, barns, and cotton gins.

The Hunlike threat sprang from Sherman the soldier, not Sherman the man. Since leaving his home in Ohio, almost all his years had been spent in Southern states or with Southern friends. The South's charm and dignity attracted Sherman the man. The South's will to resist attracted Sherman the soldier, and he took dead aim at it.

Georgia families trembled at his coming. In terror they left their corn and forage along his route. His bummers swept the land like a gigantic broom.

From the second day onward Negroes flocked to the Blue columns. Slaves walked beside the soldiers, happily toting rifles and knapsacks. They entertained by the campfires and cooked the rare dishes they had prepared for their owners. Small children were hidden in wagons, in order that they might see the land of liberty.

&

SHERMAN, who hated war, had not learned to hate slavery. If he did not welcome the Negroes, however, Northern abolitionists might accuse him of deliberately mistreating the race. Let them. Let the armchair warriors rant! He must act according to what he believed was right.

He had Negro preachers brought to him. He explained that this was not the hour of liberation. He could not care for any but his soldiers.

Although twenty-five thousand Negroes accompanied the army at one stage or another, all but six thousand soon returned to their homes as asked.

On December 12, a sea gull was sighted. On the 13th, a forward unit climbed atop a rice mill and saw a black smokestack move above the trees. A steamboat plowed the Cassabaw Sound.

Its signal flag spelled out the question: *Who are you?*

The answer flashed back, *General Sherman.*

The goal was his. He had cut himself adrift from his bases. He had beaten off the timid sorties of the enemy. He had dealt with the Negro as he thought just. He had reached the sea.

Behind him lay a swath of destruction three hundred miles long and sixty miles wide. Georgia could nourish the Southland no more.

From the coast his army swooped up into South Carolina to give the hotbed of secession a "bellyful of war."

Once Georgia and South Carolina were gutted, the Confederacy became a hollow shell. William T. Sherman, the man who served the North and loved the South, had carried peace nearer to both nations.

WILLIAM TECUMSEH SHERMAN

> Born: Lancaster, Ohio, February 8, 1820.
> Died: New York City, New York, February 14, 1891.

The Illustration, Page 189: *The destruction of Atlanta.*

George Henry Thomas
Major General, United States of America

46

THE LONELY SOUTHERNER

MAJOR GEORGE THOMAS was eager for a breath of fresh air. As his train pulled into the station of Norfolk, Virginia, he made his way to the rear platform. What happened next was one of those cruel little mischances which reshape men's lives.

Before the train had fully stopped, Thomas impatiently hopped to the ground. He lost his footing, and his massive frame plunged into a ditch with wrenching force.

Six weeks he lay in a Norfolk hospital recovering from a spine injury. For the rest of his life he was obliged to ride and walk deliberately or suffer stabbing pain. And for that he was cruelly misjudged. His careful gait was mistaken for slowness, and he was regarded as a plodder. Dependable, yes; but no man to rely upon in the swiftly rising emergencies of battle.

Unjust as was this opinion, he was to know a greater injustice. Through four years of war he would feel the weight of a question mark—his loyalty.

After leaving the hospital, Thomas and his wife journeyed to his home in Virginia. It was 1860; North and South were girding. Thomas informed his family that he could not sympathize with the disunionists.

"I might have known it," his brother grumbled bitterly. "You always had a streak of Yankee in you."

He referred to George's boyhood practice of instructing Negroes. After school, George used to repeat the day's lessons to the children of his father's slaves.

Although a traitor to his family, George Thomas stayed true to his oath to defend the United States. To a spy-jittery capital, it did not matter that he had renounced his home and his family. He was a Southerner.

Promotions stuck in the web of suspicion. The greenest peacetime lieutenant promptly received a majority or a colonelcy in the expanded wartime army. Major George Thomas, a man of forty-five, with twenty years of service, was gingerly nudged up one rank, to lieutenant colonel.

Twenty years of experience cannot be shrunk under a silver leaf. His ability quickly showed. After a month he was promoted to colonel. In August, 1861, his West Point roommate, William T. Sherman, personally vouched for his loyalty. Thomas got his overdue brigadier general's star.

The War Department watched uneasily. On January 19, 1862, the Virginian led Union troops against the Confederates at Mill Springs, Kentucky.

In the tumult of bullets he gave his orders serenely. The only sign of what he felt was his grizzly whiskers. When worried or troubled, he mussed them. When pleased, he smoothed them. At the beginning of the battle the whiskers were mussed. At the conclusion they were smooth.

Mill Springs represented the first important Union victory in the West. Had the commanding officer been anyone else, a promotion would have followed within a week. George Thomas, the slow, solid, lonely Southerner, was made to wait three months.

In October Major General Thomas was put in charge of one of the three corps of the Army of the Cumberland, under General William Rosecrans. Thomas helped drive the Confederates, led by Braxton Bragg, out of Tennessee.

Within a year Bragg was reinforced by Longstreet's corps of Virginians. Confidently, Bragg engaged the Army of the Cumberland near Chickamauga Creek in northern Georgia. On the second day of fighting, Rosecrans blundered. He removed from the line the division facing Longstreet. Longstreet called up everything and rushed into the yawning hole. Half the Union army, including general headquarters, was whirled away.

The despairing Rosecrans prepared for a last stand at Chattanooga, whither his panicked army had swept him. Suddenly a courier galloped out of the dusk. He bore a message from Rosecrans' chief of staff, Brigadier General James A. Garfield, later President of the United States.

Rosecrans read: *Thomas standing like a rock. Has seven divisions intact.*

Slow George Thomas, his line pounded into a horseshoe, his beard mussed, was holding the road to Chattanooga. Eventually he withdrew on orders. But his six-hour stand had saved the Army of the Cumberland in what was the bloodiest battle of the western theater.

Acclaim poured upon him. He was hailed as the "Rock of Chickamauga." "There is nothing finer in history than Thomas at Chickamauga . . ." a historian was to declare years afterward.

❦

THOMAS succeeded the discredited Rosecrans as chief of the Army of the Cumberland. He commanded it in the campaigns against Chattanooga and Atlanta under Sherman's direction.

Then Sherman departed for the sea, taking the cream of the western forces. The uncomplaining Thomas was left with remnants to handle the Confederates under slashing John Hood.

Thomas filled out his leftover divisions with men from beyond the Mississippi. In his ranks were Negro units. Against prevailing sentiment, he intended to use colored men as combat troops.

Nothing but Hood's total destruction would satisfy Thomas. He prepared painstakingly. Grant, holding down Lee hundreds of miles away, demanded results. As the days went by, Grant grew more and more exasperated. At last he dispatched General John Logan with an order relieving Thomas of command.

Logan never delivered the order. Before he could, Thomas went after Hood and hit him like a sledge. On December 15 and 16, 1864, near Nashville, Tennessee, Thomas' fifty-five thousand "pickup" troops inflicted upon Hood's thirty-eight thousand veterans the most terrible defeat of the war.

On the heels of the slaughter, the man who was called "too slow" pounced like a lion. His pursuit was a model of coldly efficient swiftness. Not in a hundred years had there been so thorough a "mop up." Hood's army was demolished.

When the nation was once again united, Thomas was assigned to command the Military Division of the Pacific at San Francisco, California. He heard himself mentioned as a Presidential candidate. And as a candidate for brevet lieutenant general.

He stubbornly refused to run for public office. He declined the brevet because it carried political overtones.

He was a soldier until his last day. A review of his war record suggests he was the best artillerist in either army. Be that as it may, history is clear on three things.

No other Union general was more loyal, more successful, and more sinned against than the big, uncomplaining Virginian.

Not for months after the war did his brother speak to him. His two sisters never did.

✤✤✤✤•✤•✤✤✤✤

GEORGE HENRY THOMAS

Born: Southampton County, Virginia, July 31, 1816.
Died: San Francisco, California, March 28, 1870.

The Illustration, Page 193: *Bronze cannon used by Union field artillery.*

196

Wade Hampton
Lieutenant General, Confederate States of America

47
GIANT FROM SOUTH CAROLINA

THE BLACK BEAR stopped and turned. Rearing on its hind legs, it snarled down at the pack of hounds that had chased it to the edge of the thicket.

Wade Hampton heard the sudden telltale change in the barking. He spurred his horse and arrived as the bear's heavy paws lashed out. Ordering the dogs away, Hampton leaped from the saddle and unsheathed a long knife. Armed only with the blade, he stalked in.

Sharp claws raked the air. Hampton ducked, shifted balance expertly, and flashed close. Steel thrust up and home, driven by two hundred pounds of brawn. The bear lived another half dozen seconds.

Wade wiped the red blade. Then he dug his strong fingers into the four-hundred-pound carcass and slung it across his horse.

The bear was one of eighty Wade Hampton was to kill with his knife. He hunted with the passion of a medieval baron. In truth, he lived like one. Everything desirable in life was his in abundance: breeding, good looks, power, land, and money.

The wealthiest man in South Carolina, Hampton also had large holdings in North Carolina and Mississippi. Three thousand slaves worked his plantations. His home, Millwood, was a jewel of luxury set amid two thousand acres of rich bottom land. Ten thousand books filled the library at Millwood, and its wine cellar was the pride of Dixie. To its drawing rooms flocked the great of many lands.

Being so richly endowed, Wade Hampton was a popular subject for myth makers. One insisted Hampton was so strong he could squeeze a horse between his legs until the animal groaned in pain. None who knew him would have bet the feat was beyond his strength.

When talk of secession spread through South Carolina, Hampton pleaded for peace and reason. When war came, he backed the Confederacy to his limit. He offered his cotton and himself. At forty-three, he might have had a snug desk job. Instead, he took to the field.

Partly at his own expense, he raised and equipped a legion composed of cavalry, infantry, and artillery. As its colonel, he received $198 monthly. That sum he would not have missed had it fallen from his pocket.

The young men of South Carolina's best families volunteered to serve under him. Many brought their own body servants. Throughout Hampton's Legion was a gentleman's organization. Privates walked with more swagger than if they had been officers in most other units.

Hampton had no formal military training. He learned as he fought. But he brought to war basic soldierly qualities. He was a wonderful horseman and woodsman. More important, years of directing plantation workers had developed his natural ability to command.

"I doubt if he ever read a book on tactics," declared a friend. "He had no need to. He knew how to maneuver the units of his command so as to occupy for offensive or defensive action the strongest points on the battlefield, and that is about all there is in tactics."

In battle, Hampton joined the skill of a crack marksman with the bravery of a bear killer. He rode at the front of most charges, sword drawn. His blade was straight and double-edged, forty inches long and weighed six pounds. Its extra largeness made it a weapon for a giant. With the exception of Nathan B. Forrest, Hampton probably had more hand-to-hand fights than any American general in history.

As he demonstrated his talents as a leader, more troops were put under him. On August 3, 1863, Hampton was made a major general. When Jeb Stuart was slain the following May, Hampton replaced him as chief of cavalry in Virginia, and immediately gave the corps a new look.

Stuart had a weakness for mounted action; that is, raids and charges. Hampton saw that an advantage might sometimes be gained by dismounting the troopers and fighting them on foot, as infantry.

Another difference between the two generals was noted by a captain who served under both.

"General Stuart," he said, "would attempt his work with whatever force he had at hand, and often seemed to try to accomplish a given result with the smallest possible number of men. General Hampton always tried to carry every available man to his point of operation, and the larger his force, the better he liked it.

"The advantage of this style of generalship was soon apparent. Under Stuart, stampedes were frequent. Under Hampton, they were unknown."

❧

HAMPTON had only a tattered part of Jeb's once proud force. In 1864, the Confederate Army was no longer able to wage offensive war. It was bled of men and horses. Hampton fought defensive actions.

He performed marvels. Time and again it was the cavalry that staved off defeat. On January 15, 1865, Hampton was rewarded with a commission as lieutenant general. He thus became the first of only two cavalrymen ever to achieve so high a rank in the Confederate Army. The second was Nathan B. Forrest, promoted six weeks later.

When the Gray armies surrendered, Hampton's spirit remained uncrushed. He wanted to escort President Davis into Texas and there continue the war. He failed, however, to overtake the fleeing President, and consequently abandoned the venture.

He went back to South Carolina. He had marched away the richest man in the state, if not in all the South. He returned one of the poorest.

He had seen both his sons fall, one fatally, in a single cavalry charge. His big body carried five wounds. His dead son, his wounds, his lieutenant general's uniform—all were for nothing. His fields and mansions were in ashes.

The bear hunter was forty-six, an age when few men have the strength to begin again. Wade moved into an overseer's house and started rebuilding his plantations.

Soon the ground yielded crops, and soon Wade Hampton was once more the first citizen of South Carolina. In 1878 he was elected governor, and soon afterward, United States Senator.

With his fame constantly increasing, he lost none of his level-headed modesty. Once a wartime comrade asked the old hero how many bluecoats he had killed.

"Eleven," said Hampton after a moment's thought.

The number seemed far too few. "What about the two at Trevilian?"

"Oh," answered Hampton. "I did not count them. They were running."

WADE HAMPTON

BORN: Columbia, South Carolina, March 28, 1818.
DIED: Columbia, South Carolina, April 11, 1902.

THE ILLUSTRATION, PAGE 197: *The Palmetto flag of South Carolina.*

Ely Samuel Parker
Lieutenant Colonel, United States of America

48

KEEPER OF THE WESTERN DOOR

ELIZABETH PARKER stood barelegged in the moonlit doorway. A dream had awakened her—a dream of a rainbow, of clouds parting, of pictures like the white man's writing.

Could not the dream be a prophecy? Was not Skaniadarii, the great Iroquois prophet, her forefather?

In the Council House of the Senecas she related her vision to the *djisgadataha* —the man who saw inside dreams. He told her what the dream meant. It was indeed a prophecy.

"A son will be born to you who will be distinguished among his nation as a peacemaker; he will become a white man as well as an Indian," said the *djisgadataha*. "He will be a wise white man, but he will never desert his Indian people. His sun will rise on Indian land and set on white man's land. Yet the ancient land of his ancestors will fold him in death."

Five months later a son, Ely, was born on the Tonawanda Reservation in New York. The baby would be a sachem in the League of Iroquois. By the time he was three he had learned his place in the world of white men. Any Indian, even one destined for the

201

highest council, ranked below the basest white.

Ridicule Ely bore with silent dignity. But groups like the Ogden Land Company, which cheated many Indians out of their land, roused his anger and his ambition. He resolved to learn to deal with the white man so that he might defend his people.

From the Baptist missionary schools he advanced to the Yates and Cayuga Academies. In his studies he proved himself equal to "white boys from the finest families in the land."

"No young man in school could compete with him in oratory," commented a schoolmate. She added the customary note of prejudice: "He was truly a prodigy, springing from such a slow, indolent race."

By the time he quit school at eighteen, Ely had argued the claims of his people in the state and federal capitals. Attired in buckskin and a hat of doeskin and feathers, he became a favorite of distinguished men. Daniel Webster, Henry Clay, and John Calhoun welcomed his company. He dined at the White House with President Polk.

Already he was fulfilling the prophecy of his mother's dream. During the next twenty years he was to defend the rights of his people. No pure-blooded Indian ever accomplished so much in a white man's culture.

For three years Parker studied law. As he prepared for admission to the bar, he made a cruel discovery. Indians were not citizens; hence the law excluded him from practicing.

Heartsick with disappointment, he changed the means to his goal. He took a short, basic course in civil engineering at Rensselaer Polytechnic Institute. By tireless work, he achieved success.

Since the age of twenty-one he had been a chief of the Senecas. His tribal name, Donehogawa, meant *Keeper of the Western Door* of the Long House. While supervising whites on the Erie Canal, Ely Parker was the leading officer of the Senecas and one of fifty sachems of the Iroquois League of Six Nations.

In 1857 he became a superintendent of construction for government projects in Galena, Illinois. Here he formed a fast friendship with the clerk of the local leather shop.

THE TOWERING round-faced Indian chief and the stocky, rock-hard clerk had three things in common. Both had engineering educations, both loved horses, and both cherished silence.

Theirs was an unlikely but a lifelong friendship.

With the outbreak of war, Parker determined to fight for the Union. True to his upbringing, he asked his father's permission. William Parker, a pensioned veteran of the War of 1812, meditated all night. In the morning he gave his blessing.

After a feast in his honor, Parker entrained for Albany. Brimming with hope, he asked for a commission and detailed his engineering background. The governor was blunt. There was no room for him.

Stunned, Parker offered his services to Secretary of State Seward.

"The war must be settled by white men only," Seward told him. "Go home, cultivate your land. We will settle our own troubles without Indian aid."

Ely Parker went back to his farm on the reservation. He had lost the bark cabin of his birth through a cunning treaty. He had been denied the right to practice law. He had been rejected for military service. All because he was a red man.

The chief of the Senecas did not sulk. He donned work clothes and plowed his fields, painted a tall pole, and floated the American flag. He would grow the food the soldiers ate.

One day in May of 1863 a soldier galloped down the road. He handed Parker a formal document—a captain's commission in the United States Army. Secretary Seward had relented.

Captain Parker joined General J. E. Smith as an engineer of the 7th Division. While at Vicksburg, Mississippi, he encountered an old friend. U. S. Grant, the leather store clerk, was a general. Parker was assigned to his staff as an assistant adjutant general.

Throughout the ensuing campaigns, Parker was as close to Grant's side as anyone. The Indian chief followed the West Pointer in and out of danger. Both had the same granite disregard of death.

The best penman on Grant's staff was Lieutenant Colonel Parker. He copied the surrender terms at Appomattox and stood beside Grant and Lee.

Afterward, he continued as Grant's military secretary. By March, 1867, he had attained the rank of brigadier general. He was declared fit, albeit an Indian, for citizenship.

Among Grant's first appointments as President was the one naming Parker Commissioner of Indian Affairs. The giant Seneca chief resigned this post in 1871, saddened by false charges of defrauding the government.

His last years were spent in the New York City police department as architect and supply clerk. He died at his summer home in Fairfield, Connecticut.

Later, his remains were reinterred on ground where seventy years before Elizabeth Parker had the vision of her unborn son.

So was the prophecy fulfilled. Donehogawa had walked far on the white man's trail. At its end, the ancient land of his ancestors folded him in death.

ELY SAMUEL PARKER

BORN: Indian Falls, New York, 1828.
DIED: Fairfield, Connecticut, August 31, 1895.

THE ILLUSTRATION, PAGE 201: *An Indian chief's head dress and Union officer's cap.*

John Wilkes Booth
Actor-Assassin

49

INTRUDER IN BOX 7

AT NINE-THIRTY on the night of April 14, 1865, John Wilkes Booth rode a rented bay mare down the stone alley behind the Ford Opera House. It was his second trip to the theater within three hours.

On his first visit he had spent some time in the Presidential box. He had cut a niche in the wall running perpendicular to the outer door. Through the inner door he had bored a peephole.

By the stage entrance he handed the mare's reins to Johnny "Peanuts," a slow-witted boy, and stepped inside.

The play, a comedy entitled *Our American Cousin*, had been in progress an hour.

Booth whispered to his fellow actors, smiled, bowed, and sidled toward the stage. From the wings he peered up into Boxes 7 and 8, which overlooked the stage. It was impossible to see anything in the darkness beyond the footlights. Because of its forward position, the flag-draped double box had the privacy of a tomb.

After a while Booth quit staring and left the theater. Being familiar with the play, he knew when the stage would be nearly empty. He had about forty minutes.

He sauntered into Taltavul's next door and fortified himself with a bottle of whisky. As he drank, two men joined a third farther down at the bar.

The newcomers were Francis Burns and Charles Forbes. They were coachman and footman respectively of the carriage which had conveyed the President to the theater. The third man was John F. Parker, thirty-four, an irresponsible member of the police force.

Parker had been assigned a post inside the theater. Growing interested in the play, he had deserted his post to watch. In ten minutes he was bored. So he walked from the theater in quest of a drink.

The post which he had deserted was outside the President's box. As Lincoln's bodyguard, his duty was to defend the President at the risk of his own life. John F. Parker, unfortunately, had never been troubled much by a sense of duty. So shortly before 10:00 P.M. the box stood unprotected.

Several women recognized Booth as he leaned at the bar. Even in this moment his vanity demanded he acknowledge their wishful glances. He smiled his gorgeous smile. Ever since he could remember, women had adored him on sight.

Had he ever bothered to study his craft, he might have surpassed as an actor his distinguished brother, Edwin Booth. Even so, John Wilkes Booth had made as much as twenty thousand dollars a year playing in small towns. Never one for remembering his lines, he got by on good looks and athletic prancing.

Now he had a part that would lift him above Edwin, above all the actors of the American stage.

He finished his whisky, paid, and strolled back to the theater. The ticket taker, Joseph Buckingham, was pleased to see the slim, likable young man. Booth entertained "Buck" with a few stories. Offhandedly, he asked the hour.

There was a profound reason for checking. Booth wanted to time his deed with those of two accomplices, who would attempt to murder Vice President Johnson and Secretary of State Seward.

Learning he was on schedule, Booth passed into the theater. His spurs twinkled in the gaslight as he ascended the stairs to the dress circle.

No more would he have to explain why he did not fight for the South he loved. No more would he have to bear the sly winks when he said, "I promised my mother I would not."

Between him and lasting fame stood Lincoln's bodyguards—he knew not how many. Accustomed to getting his own way, he felt quite confident. His charm and his position as an actor would admit him to the presence of his victim. If not, he had a dagger.

The balcony was deserted. Unbelievable . . .

ैस

SOFTLY Booth opened the first of the two doors behind the President of the United States.

He worked methodically. He secured the door against a chance incomer by bracing an iron bar between the door panel and the niche he had cut earlier in the wall. He put his eye to the peephole behind the playgoers.

Lincoln sat in a comfortable haircloth rocking chair, Mrs. Lincoln at his right. Major Henry Reed Rathbone was nearer the stage beside his fiancée, Clara Harris.

Booth gripped a small, eight-ounce brass derringer; it had but one shot. With his left hand he pulled out the dagger.

He scorned to mask his classic features. To be recognized was in keeping with his concept of the drama. He wished everyone to know him as a patriot, as the man who slew the oppressor and avenged his country.

In the past six months he might have slain Lincoln on the street almost any night and fled. But he did not consider himself a "common cutthroat." He had deliberately waited until Lincoln attended the theater. Seventeen hundred persons were about to see enacted the immortal death scene of the American stage. And he, John Wilkes Booth, was author, director, and star.

He pushed open the inner door.

Unhurriedly, he sighted along his outstretched arm. With the muzzle five feet from his graying head, he squeezed the trigger.

Major Rathbone rushed from his chair and received a knife slash across his right arm. Booth tossed away the derringer and sprang onto the railing. In the twelve-foot drop to the stage, he snagged his spur in a draped flag and landed on all fours. His left leg, slightly in advance, snapped two inches above the ankle.

"*Sic semper tyrannis!*" he shouted, scrambling up and waving the dagger, red with the blood of Major Rathbone. "The South is avenged!"

The audience gasped, uncertain yet vaguely sensing a horror. Booth limped off the stage. Sixty seconds from the time he had fired the shot, he hauled himself upon the bay mare and galloped from Washington.

Abraham Lincoln died the next morning without regaining consciousness. No man's death could have been less desired by true patriots of the Confederacy. With Lincoln died the great hope of the South for a generous peace.

Three of the conspirators, including the pair who failed to kill Seward and Johnson, were caught and hanged. Booth, the ringleader, was tracked to a barn in Virginia and shot in the neck.

Dying, he remained aware that he was acting out his greatest role. His last words were delivered for the closing curtain.

"Tell mother I died for my country."

JOHN WILKES BOOTH

BORN: Bel Air, Maryland, 1838.
DIED: Garrett's Barn, Virginia, April 26, 1865.

THE ILLUSTRATION, PAGE 205: *Ford's Theatre and the playbill of the night of Lincoln's assassination.*

Robert Edward Lee
General, Confederate States of America

50

GREAT GENTLEMAN

SOMETHING STRANGE hung in the air above the leaning fields. The cannon were silent, the rattle of carbines had died out. From the thin Confederate lines the generals were quietly disappearing.

General Lee, trailed by three of his staff, rode toward the village of Appomattox Courthouse. Along his route were gaunt and silent men, the faithful of four years of war. They looked at their commanding general with uneasy wonder.

An artilleryman, William Owen, observed Lee's attire. He was in full uni-

form, "with handsome embroidered belt and dress sword, tall hat, and buff gauntlets."

All this finery, thought Owen, was ominous. General Lee normally campaigned in a gray sack coat with side pockets, "quite like the costume of a businessman in cities."

The general dismounted by the Appomattox to water Traveller, his charger. When the dappled gray finished drinking, the little cavalcade continued on toward the village. A colonel trotted ahead to locate a suitable building. Grant had left it up to

General Lee to select a meeting place.

The house chosen was a modest brick dwelling faced by a white wooden porch. It belonged to Wilmer McLean. Lee entered the center hall and turned left into a front room, the parlor. He seated himself by a window, laid his hat and gauntlets on a small oval table, and waited.

Half an hour later, at 1:30 P.M., Ulysses Grant arrived in a rough, mud-spattered uniform. The Union commander greeted Lee courteously, remarking they had met once before, in the Mexican War.

"Yes," replied Lee, who in Mexico proved himself the finest combat officer in the United States Army. "I have often tried to recollect how you looked," he said to the younger man, "but I have never been able to recall a single feature."

The conversation rambled pleasantly. Members of Grant's staff were invited into the parlor. They came in softly, self-consciously, "like men entering a sick chamber."

Lee nodded at General Seth Williams, an old friend. Once more the talk wandered. Lee reined it in. "I suppose, General Grant, that the object of our meeting is fully understood."

Grant spoke earnestly of his desire for peace. Lee requested that the terms be written out. The Union commander lighted a pipe. He wrote steadily in a manifold order book prepared to imprint three copies. After going over the words with Ely Parker, his military secretary, he passed the book to Lee.

Thirty-nine years of military service spun down to two pages of pencil scratches in an order book.

Lee removed his steel-rimmed eyeglasses from his pocket. Very deliberately, perhaps to cover his tenseness, he wiped the lenses. His new boots squeaked as he crossed his legs. He set the eyeglasses on his nose, picked up the book, and began to read Grant's words.

. . . *I propose to receive the surrender of the Army of Northern Virginia . . .*

THE ARMY of Northern Virginia! For thirty-four months Robert E. Lee had been its brain, its power, and its soul. In all that time he had not once had a force equal to the Union's—the blue-coated Americans he called "those people," never "the enemy." Against odds as high as three to one, he had wrung his victories. Now only one-third of his men were armed; hundreds were without shoes and blankets. To fight on was futile.

Although beaten, although aged beyond any man in either army by the conflict, Lee still commanded a situation. After reading Grant's first page, he corrected a minor error. Turning the leaf, he noted the sentence permitting the officers to retain their arms, horses, and baggage.

"This will have a very happy effect upon my army," he said.

Grant did not acknowledge the compliment. "Unless," he asserted firmly, "you have some suggestions to make in regard to the form in which I have stated the terms, I will have a copy of the letter made in ink and sign it."

"There is one thing I would like to mention," Lee answered carefully. "The cavalrymen and artillerymen in our army own their own horses. Our organization differs from yours. I would like to understand whether these men will be permitted to retain their horses."

Grant was surprised to learn of the Confederate system. Certainly the soldiers might keep their horses and mules "to work their little farms."

"This will have the best possible effect upon my men!" Lee observed. Then, gravely, he remarked that his men had not eaten much but parched corn for the past few days.

Grant promptly directed his quartermaster to deliver twenty-five thousand rations to the Confederates.

There was a smattering of conversation. Grant boyishly apologized for his rough garb which contrasted with Lee's ceremonial magnificence. He introduced his officers...

All at once there was nothing more to say. Lee shook hands with Grant, bowed to the others, and left the room. None who stood in his presence would forget him. Afterward, a Northern officer recalled:

"His manners and bearing were perfect and stamped him a thoroughbred gentleman . . . that happy blending of dignity and courtesy so difficult to describe . . . no haughtiness or ill-humor betrayed on the one hand; nor affected cheerfulness, forced politeness nor flippancy on the other. He was a gentleman —which fully and wholly expresses his behavior."

On the porch Lee returned the salutes of the Union soldiers wearily but politely. He pulled on his gauntlets, gazing beyond the valley to where his tattered army camped on a hill.

It was four o'clock, April 9, 1865. Robert E. Lee, son of George Washington's chief of artillery, husband of Martha Washington's great-granddaughter, gentleman and first citizen of the Confederacy, was ready to yield his place in the hall of giants.

Ahead were promises of easy riches. He would refuse them, accepting instead the presidency of Washington College at Lexington, Virginia. His salary: fifteen hundred dollars a year. His reason: to train young men to do their duty in peace as he had trained them to do their duty in war.

And he would urge the South to abandon the dream of the Confederacy and support a reunited government. By his words would he urge it, and by his example.

He smote his gloved hands together as he stood on the porch of the McLean house. In a voice that nearly failed him, he called to his orderly for his charger.

Traveller was led out. Lee mounted, and as he lowered into the saddle there broke "unguardedly from his lips a long deep sigh, almost a moan."

Then he pulled the reins gently and rode off toward his little army and the sunlight.

ROBERT EDWARD LEE

Born: Stratford, Virginia, January 19, 1807.
Died: Lexington, Virginia, October 12, 1870.

The Illustration, Page 209: *General Lee's letter to General Grant April 9, 1865, and the "Stars and Bars," the flag of the Confederacy.*

TWO flags flying.

Now one flag was coming down. The war was ending at Appomattox Courthouse.

General Grant's terms had been given. General Lee's aide was copying a letter of acceptance for his signature.

As the pen scratched, low conversations began in the McLean parlor. Grant introduced his officers.

Lee shook hands without a change of expression. Then he was introduced to Lieutenant Colonel Ely S. Parker.

The Virginian apparently took his first notice of the Iroquois chief. His eyebrows rose as, for several seconds, he stared at Parker's swarthy features.

The Union generals shifted uneasily. One thought Lee believed Grant was deliberately trying to humiliate him with a Negro. Another feared the aristocratic Southerner, an old Indian fighter, was insulted by the presence of a member of a savage race.

Neither surmise was true.

The truth was a reaffirmation of the humility of two great men and of a fundamental principle of our nation.

Robert E. Lee graciously extended his hand. "I am glad to see one real American here," he said.

"General Lee," Parker said softly, "we are all Americans."

A CALENDAR OF CONFLICT

1859	OCTOBER 16	John Brown's raid at Harper's Ferry, Virginia (now West Virginia). (Chapters 1 and 3)
1860	DECEMBER 20	South Carolina adopts Ordinance of Secession.
1861	JANUARY 9	Mississippi secedes.
	JANUARY 10	Florida secedes.
	JANUARY 11	Alabama secedes.
	JANUARY 19	Georgia secedes.
	JANUARY 26	Louisiana secedes.
	FEBRUARY 1	Texas secedes.
	FEBRUARY 4	Confederate States of America established at Montgomery, Alabama.
	FEBRUARY 9	Jefferson Davis elected provisional President of the Confederate States of America.
	FEBRUARY 18	Davis inaugurated as President of the Confederacy at Montgomery.
	MARCH 4	Abraham Lincoln inaugurated as President of the United States of America at Washington, D.C.
	APRIL 12-13	The bombardment of Fort Sumter, at Charleston, South Carolina. (Chapters 1 and 3)
	APRIL 15	Lincoln calls for 75,000 three-month volunteers. (Chapter 2)
	APRIL 17	Virginia secedes.
	APRIL 19	Baltimore mobs riot against Union troops on way to Washington, D.C. (Chapter 17)
		Lincoln proclaims blockade of South. (Chapter 30)
	MAY 6	Arkansas secedes.
	MAY 7	Tennessee secedes.
	MAY 20	North Carolina secedes.
	JULY 20	First Battle of Bull Run (Manassas), Virginia. (Chapters 4 and 5)
	JULY 21	Transfer of the capital of the Confederacy from Montgomery to Richmond, Virginia completed. (Chapter 6)
	AUGUST 10	Battle of Wilson's Creek, Missouri.
	NOVEMBER 7	Union fleet and troops capture Port Royal, South Carolina.
1862	FEBRUARY 6	Union troops capture Fort Henry, Tennessee.
	FEBRUARY 14-16	Union troops capture Fort Donelson, Tennessee. (Chapter 37)
	MARCH 6-8	Battle of Pea Ridge, Arkansas (including Bentonville, Leetown, and Elkorn Tavern).
	MARCH 9	Battle of *Merrimack* and *Monitor*. (Chapter 7)

1862	MARCH-JULY	Peninsula Campaign (including Fair Oaks, Seven Days), Virginia. (Chapters 10 and 14)
	MARCH-JUNE	Valley Campaign, Virginia. (Chapters 10, 14 and 26)
	APRIL 6-7	Battle of Shiloh (Pittsburgh Landing), Tennessee.
	APRIL 12	Locomotive chase in Georgia. (Chapter 8)
	APRIL 13	*Planter* stolen by Negro crew in Charleston Harbor, South Carolina. (Chapter 11)
	APRIL 24-25	Union fleet captures New Orleans. (Chapter 9)
	JUNE 6	Memphis, Tennessee captured by Union forces.
	JUNE 12	Stuart rides around McClellan in Virginia. (Chapter 12)
	AUGUST 29-30	Second Battle of Bull Run (Manassas), Virginia.
	SEPTEMBER 16-17	Battle of Sharpsburg (Antietam), Maryland. (Chapters 14, 15, 16 and 20)
	OCTOBER 8	Battle of Perryville, Kentucky.
	DECEMBER 13	Battle of Fredericksburg, Virginia. (Chapter 16)
	DECEMBER 31— JAN. 2, 1863	Battle of Stone's River (Murfreesboro), Tennessee.
1863	FEBRUARY 9	Fairfax Courthouse raided by Mosby's Rangers (Chapter 19)
	FEBRUARY 12	Chase-Sprague wedding climaxes Washington's wartime social calendar. (Chapter 32)
	FEBRUARY 26	Dummy ironclad rules portion of Mississippi River. (Chapter 18)
	APRIL 16—JULY 4	Siege of Vicksburg, Mississippi. (Chapter 28)
	MAY 1-4	Battle of Chancellorsville, Virginia. (Chapters 10 and 26)
	JULY 1-3	Battle of Gettysburg, Pennsylvania. (Chapters 27 and 31)
	JULY 2-26	Morgan's raid into Kentucky, Indiana and Ohio. (Chapter 23)
	JULY 13-15	New York City draft riots. (Chapter 29)
	SEPTEMBER 19-20	Battle of Chickamauga, Georgia. (Chapter 46)
	NOVEMBER 17— DECEMBER 4	Knoxville, Tennessee besieged by Union troops.
	NOVEMBER 24-25	Battle of Chattanooga, Tennessee (including Lookout Mountain and Missionary Ridge).
1864	FEBRUARY 9	Mass escape of Union officers from Libby Prison, Richmond, Virginia. (Chapter 33)
	FEBRUARY 17	*Housatonic* sunk by submarine. (Chapter 34)
	FEBRUARY 28— MARCH 4	Kilpatrick-Dahlgren raid to Richmond, Virginia. (Chapter 36)

A CALENDAR OF CONFLICT, *Continued*

1864 APRIL 8-9   Red River Campaign ends at Pleasant Hill, Louisiana. (Chapter 38)

MAY-JUNE   Wilderness Campaign, Virginia (including Wilderness, May 5-6; Spotsylvania, May 8-18; and Cold Harbor, June 1-3).

JUNE 5   Siege of Petersburg, Virginia starts (lasting until April 2, 1865).

JUNE 19   Battle of *Alabama* and *Kearsarge* off Cherbourg, France. (Chapter 13)

JUNE 27   Battle of Kenesaw Mountain, Georgia.

JULY 11   Confederate troops reach gates to Washington, D.C. (Chapters 35 and 40)

JULY 22—
   SEPTEMBER 2   Siege of Atlanta, Georgia.

AUGUST 5-23   Union fleet sails into Mobile Bay and assists Union troops in capture of Fort Gaines and Fort Morgan, Alabama.

OCTOBER 19   Confederate raiders occupy St. Albans, Vermont. (Chapter 42)
         Battle of Cedar Creek, Virginia. (Chapters 40 and 41)

OCTOBER 28   *Albemarle* destroyed in Roanoke River, North Carolina. (Chapter 43)

NOVEMBER 8   Lincoln re-elected President of the United States. (Chapters 14 and 44)

NOVEMBER 15—
   DECEMBER 13   Sherman's march to the sea (Chapter 45)

NOVEMBER 29   Battle of Spring Hill, Tennessee.

NOVEMBER 30   Battle of Franklin, Tennessee.

DECEMBER 10-21   Siege of Savannah, Georgia.

DECEMBER 15-16   Battle of Nashville, Tennessee. (Chapter 46)

1865 MARCH 19-21   Battle of Bentonville, North Carolina.

APRIL 9   General Lee surrenders the Army of Northern Virginia at Appomattox, Virginia. (Chapters 48 and 50)

APRIL 14   President Lincoln assassinated at Washington, D.C. (Chapters 37, 44 and 49)

APRIL 26   General Johnston surrenders Army of Tennessee and other units at Durham Station, North Carolina. (Chapter 22)

MAY   Surrender of the remaining Confederate forces.

JUNE 8   Grand Review of Union forces, Washington, D.C. (Chapter 21)

NOTE: Kentucky and Missouri remained in the Union, but "representatives" were recognized by the Confederate Congress and thus these states were claimed by the Confederacy.

ACKNOWLEDGMENTS

The author wishes to express his gratitude to:

Miss Muriel Fuller, of New York, for an adroit blue pencil.

Mrs. August E. Wilkoc, Mrs. George F. Smith, and Mrs. Harold E. Hulme of the Eastchester Public Library, New York; Mrs. Elizabeth C. Martin, Mrs. Katharine Gardner, and Mrs. Catherine Scott of the Bronxville Public Library, New York; and Miss Frances Elrod of the Mount Vernon Public Library, New York, for generous, patient, and invaluable help.

Burke Davis of Greensboro, North Carolina, Arnold Gates of Garden City, New York, Irving Werstein and Philip Van Doren Stern, of New York City, Guy C. Coulombe of Staten Island, New York, John C. Varelmann of Cincinnati, Ohio, Miss Celeste Slauson of Hackensack, New Jersey, Colonel Allen P. Julian of Atlanta, Georgia, and Alan T. Nolan of Indianapolis, Indiana, for advice on episodes and biographies.

Dr. Howard Simon of White Plains, New York, for the freedom to mine in his rare book collection; Dr. Robert S. Holzman of New York University, New York City, for material on Sally Tompkins; Mrs. Dorothy Sterling of Rye, New York, for material on Robert Smalls; Harry Wagner Acton of Old Saybrook, Connecticut, for information about Thomas Acton.

R. N. Williams, 2nd, director, Historical Society of Pennsylvania, for information about Colonel Thomas Rose and Colonel Ulric Dahlgren; G. Glenn Clift, of the Kentucky Historical Society, for information about Lieutenant Bennett H. Young; John Melville Jennings, Director of the Virginia Historical Society, and Miss Dorothy C. Barck, of the New York State Historical Association, for information about Jedediah Hotchkiss.